My husband and I served years of our marriage whi for mentoring and wisdom from other seasoned women in the ministry who could not only relate to my daily experiences but be inspiring voices to help and encourage me through the challenges of being a pastor's wife. I would have been eternally grateful for a devotional book like Love, Joy, & Faithfulness, A 90-Day Devotional for the Pastor's Wife. I challenge you to allow its pages to speak into your life and feed your soul.

Ellen Tuttle, teacher; speaker; wife of Phil Tuttle, President of *Walk Thru the Bible*

Every pastor's wife needs encouragement, help and wisdom to help her thrive in her God-given role. Flowers for the Pastor's Wife *is just such a resource, one for which I'm incredibly thankful.*

Christine Hoover, author of *The Church Planting Wife* & *How to Thrive as a Pastor's Wife*

Serving as a pastor's wife is a joy and privilege, but it can also be a challenging and lonely experience. That's why I am so grateful for the Flowers for the Pastor's Wife *ministry. By providing community, support, and encouragement, Flowers helps ministry wives grow closer to God, be renewed in their faith, and continue to lovingly serve their churches and communities. I highly recommend their ministry.*

Leigh Powers, author of *Renewed: A 40 Day Devotional for Healing from Church Hurt and Loving Well in Ministry*

This is a devotional written by small-town pastors' wives for small-town pastors' wives. They understand the unique pressures and blessings involved. They have written from the perspective of living with, caring for, and loving the flock God has entrusted to them.

Roxy Klassen, wife of Ron Klassen, Director of
Rural Home Missionary Association

Flowers for the Pastor's Wife *aims to fill a void for pastors' wives. It is a safe place to ask questions, gain perspective, seek prayer support, and gently remind yourself that your ministry is not about you: it is about the Lord. If you have felt the loneliness of being unable to share transparently about the details of your suffering, if you've known the difficulty of supporting your husband through trials, if you've longed for someone who really understands and can relate to the unique struggles that a ministry family faces, the* Flowers Ministry *can help.*

Stacey Weeks, author of *Glorious Surrender*
& *Chasing Holiness*

As I see all that is happening with Flowers for the Pastor's Wife: *the blogs, the Facebook group, the online chats and discussion, and now this devotional book, I wish that this had been available when I was a young pastor's wife. There was no help for us and little contact with other pastors' wives. It is such a pleasure to be able to recommend* Flowers for the Pastor's Wife *to other small-town and rural-church pastors' wives. May it continue to be a blessing to pastors' wives across North America and around the world.*

Gloria Johnston M.T.S, Administrative Assistant
Small Church Connections

Love, Joy & Faithfulness

A 90-Day Devotional

Flowers for the Pastor's Wife

Flowers Publishing

For more information please visit:
Flowers for the Pastor's Wife: smalltownpastorswives.com
Facebook: www.facebook.com/FlowersforthePastorsWife
Instagram: Flowersforthepastors_wife
Pinterest: flowersforthepastorswife
Twitter: FlowersforthePW

Love, Joy & Faithfulness

A 90-Day Devotional

Table of Contents

Preface

*M*y father was a pastor for 53 years and my husband a youth pastor for 18 years. Now both my husband, Bob, and I train women and men to serve the church. My oldest daughter was in high school when, for the first time in my life, I belonged to a church where neither my daddy nor my husband was the pastor. It was then I realized more fully the gift it is to be the pastor's wife.

I remember when it hit me that this was the first church I ever attended that did not welcome my family with a party the first Sunday we showed up! No one expected me to care for them; no one automatically gave me a place to serve. It was then that I deeply appreciated the gift it is when people easily accept love and ministry from you just because you are married to the pastor. Being a pastor's wife is one of my favorite gifts from the Lord.

No, it did not always feel like a gift. I struggled with discouragement, weariness, and times of nagging incongruence between what "they" thought my faith was and what I knew about my heart struggles. Criticism of my husband or broken friendships with women in the church could be levelling. More than once, my love for Jesus Christ's church was tested.

In this book are devotionals written with you in mind. The hope is that each day you will draw your eyes and heart to Jesus and find Him through His Word. He is always with you in the places to which you are called. The strengthening gift of this book is to point you to the One who is the Giver of all gifts, both great and small.

Dr. Pamela McRae

Dr. Pam MacRae has been involved in ministry to women in both church and parachurch settings for over 30 years. She frequently speaks at conferences and retreats and is currently a professor at Moody Bible Institute where she oversees the Ministry to Women and Ministry to Victims of Sexual Exploitation majors. Pam earned her MAMin from Moody Theological Seminary and her DMin from Bethel Seminary. Pam and her husband, Bob, who is also a professor at Moody, have two married daughters and six grandchildren.

Prayer of Dedication

*L*ord, thank You for Your Word!

Fill us with Your thoughts so that our lives will reflect Your love.

Lord, as pastors' wives, we try to handle many things at the same time. Help us to cling tightly to You in our struggles and hard circumstances, knowing that our joy comes from You.

Lord, cause us to not grow weary of doing good. Help us to not feel defeated. Strengthen us so that we can be faithful.

Prompt us to pursue Christ so that we can experience His love, joy, and faithfulness.

In His name we ask all these things, Amen.

Mel Boyle

This book contains selections from our blog, *Flowers for the Pastor's Wife*. We pray that these devotionals will encourage you as you serve God in supporting both your families and your congregations.

Letter to a Pastor's Wife

*D*ear Pastor's Wife,

You feel unsure. The big fish in your little pond have loud voices, but there's hope in the hardship. God is at work.

Sins committed against you might break your heart, but the truly devastating sins will be the ones you commit against others in the name of self-preservation. God will reveal shocking roots of pride, selfishness, and a fear of man. He will call you to humble repentance.

It could be years before some scars heal, decades for others. But if you seek the Lord more than you seek validation, acceptance, or getting your way, you will learn contentment. Days where you relied on your own strength and wisdom and where you forged your own way will be redeemed. You'll learn the strange lesson that improved circumstances, higher attendance, or filled offering plates do not bring contentment. <u>Contentment isn't a feeling; it is a choice. It is a choice to rejoice in the goodness of God because your joy is found in Him, not circumstances.</u>

You'll trust your heart to untrustworthy people and get hurt. You'll unintentionally hurt others. You'll believe the lie that intimate friendships are not possible for the pastor's wife. You'll long to be known, but you'll resist transparency. You'll take far too long to learn that isolation is not a safe place. When sacrificing friendship and community becomes too costly, you'll reach out again. But this time, let wisdom remind you that only Jesus loves perfectly.

Dark days will overwhelm you, but you will also be overwhelmed with the privilege of being used by God, overwhelmed by His grace, and overwhelmed by His love. You'll absorb hits from the enemy, but you'll get back up because your life is God's life. Your church is His church. It is His ministry, and you are His daughter to use as He sees fit. The thought will both scare you and comfort you in a strange and intimate dance. You'll eventually accept that God has used every struggle to sanctify you, stretch you, and solidify your faith. That will drive you to your knees in gratitude.

Your black-and-white world will accept grey in some areas but not in others. You'll come full circle and discover that some things are black and white after all. You'll learn to pray, wearing God's armor and waging war against the forces of darkness. You'll learn that all-in, authentic, humble, and God-centered prayer brings glory to God in a way that periodic, request-based, I-need-God-to-perform prayer cannot. It's going to get messy, but remember that Jesus is building His church, and the gates of Hell will not prevail against it (Matthew 16:18).

Stay strong, sweet sister. Don't expect easy. Expect God. He is worth it.

Stacey Weeks

Love

Let all that you do be done in love.

1 Corinthians 16:14

*W*hen asked about the first attribute that comes to mind to describe God, many would say out of habit, "God is love," even if they don't really understand it in the face of a broken world.

Whether we grew up in a home with a loving earthly father or not, we believe in God's love, and we yearn to experience the deep, abiding love that Scripture describes. This is the un-conditional, never-changing, endless kind of love we were wired for at creation when He made us in His own image— the kind of love we long for in our childhood home, romanti-cize about for our marriages, try to emulate for our children, and live out in our churches.

We know this love because we've experienced it on some level. It defines us as believers. It characterizes us as authentic and legitimate members of the Body of Christ. It is the all-en-compassing purpose which drives us to embrace our calling, our relationships, our hardships—even our failings. It's what spurs us on to greater good, to take the high road, to speak kindly or not at all.

It allows us to speak truth effectively, to forgive and to recon-cile, to withhold judgment and to extend grace. It defies all sense and logic. Love is the reason and purpose for which God made us. They will know us by our love.

In this section of the devotional, we consider love—God's love—His love for us as well as our love for Him and for oth-ers. As you read, may you feel God's embrace and hear Him whisper, "I love you, my daughter."

Ellen Tuttle

Let Go and Hold Fast *1*

For the love of Christ controls us, because we have concluded this: that one has died for all, therefore all have died; and he died for all, that those who live might no longer live for themselves but for him who for their sake died and was raised.

2 Corinthians 5:14-15

*H*ow do you catch a monkey? Put a treat in a hole in the ground just large enough for him to get his hand through. Because the monkey doesn't want to let go of the treat, he will be trapped. Then…you've got him!

This is a perfect picture of how God's Word challenges us to not hold too tightly to the things we love, but to remember that the love of Christ holds us fast to Him. As the verse above says, "For the love of Christ controls us."

The Greek word used for *control* is translated "to hold completely, to hold fast, to hold together in a whole so that no pieces fall." It makes me think of gluing a puzzle together so it can be hung on the wall. God holds us together without glue—this is the love that holds us fast!

Why is this so important for us to remember? It is because we hold too tightly to things other than Christ—to our marriages, our children, our reputations, our recreational activities, our service in the church—and become trapped into serving ourselves instead of serving God.

His love for us should compel us to do everything for Him instead of keeping a tight grip on these things for our selfish aims. The self-sacrificing love of Christ is our example.

His secure love compels us to no longer live for ourselves, to stop holding tightly to those things we feel are important to our security, and to then live for the One who died and rose again, giving us victory over sin and death. Praise His name!

How can the monkey get free? By simply letting go. We must do the same — let go of lesser things, and take that next step of holding fast to Him.

Wendy McCready

Lord, I confess that I deceive myself into thinking I am in control of things. Give me grace to let go and to trust You, to be controlled by Your love alone. Amen.

In this the love of God was made manifest among us, that God sent his only Son into the world, so that we might live through him. ...No one has ever seen God; if we love one another, God abides in us and his love is perfected in us.

1 John 4:9, 12

*W*e once walked through premarital counselling with a wonderful couple. In true small-town spirit, he has been a long-time attender of our church, and she is a teacher in the local school district.

In our sessions, my husband repeatedly mentioned 1 John 4:9-12. Trying to explain the mystery of marital love and God's love is challenging. We don't always have the words to explain, and unless you have witnessed and experienced it, you can't begin to understand. But this passage teaches us how to treat one another and from where we are to draw our strength in relationships.

We've all heard sermons about how God loved us so much that He sent Christ to die for our sins, but verse twelve explains that nobody has seen God, so we don't have a visual example from Him of how to love people. Because the Holy Spirit of God resides in us and guides us, and because of the endless and boundless love of God, a natural by-product is that we love one another with the same outpouring of love.

By God's love being perfected in us, love is continually renewed and can overflow to others. That doesn't mean we will always have everlasting patience with difficult people, but because of God's love and forgiveness, we have God's love available to share. It doesn't mean that we will never face trials, but because God's love is full of grace and mercy, we know that His love in us produces the character we need to grow and endure during that time.

I can love because of God's love abiding in me. It's not my love to give or to take away. It's God's love, and He faithfully gives us more and more. So, when we meet with engaged couples, we'll keep talking to all of them about the abounding love of God and how He faithfully provides everything we need in marriage and beyond, more than we can do or expect from each other in our own strength.

Cara Kipp

Dear Lord, give us the strength to love with a heart as big and deep as Yours. Help us to have patience with those around us. We look to You to guide our hearts, minds, and actions. Amen.

Bear one another's burdens, and so fulfill the law of Christ.

Galatians 6:2

*W*hen lifting weights, it is necessary to have a trustworthy spotter—someone you can depend on to catch the weight if it becomes too much to bear. Being a pastor's wife is like being your husband's spotter, someone your husband can depend on to help bear ministry burdens—a confidante. Ministry burdens come at pastors at all times, and sometimes, it is just too much to bear alone.

Galatians 6:2 tells us to bear one another's burdens. When ministry burdens threaten to suffocate my husband, I need to help bear the weight alongside him. This can mean listening, offering advice, crying together over brokenness, and ultimately, working together to bring these burdens to Christ. It means praying for God's healing, comfort, and guidance for ourselves and for others.

As my husband's confidante, it is crucial that I am completely trustworthy. My husband doesn't share every piece of information with me (nor should he), but he often seeks my opinion and advice in difficult situations. Doing so means he trusts me to have absolute discretion.

Confidentiality can be difficult to maintain in the church (especially in a small, rural church). People will ask me if I know about a certain situation, and I have to say, "That isn't something I can talk about." It can also be tempting to treat people differently because of confidential knowledge. I have to determine beforehand that I will respond with the love of Christ, in spite of what I now know about an individual's circumstances or decisions.

The most important part of my role as spotter is to remember that, just as my husband isn't strong enough to hold these burdens alone, I'm not strong enough to take them from him. I can help carry them, but we both need to remember to turn to Christ for rest and that His burden is light. If we turn to Him, He can give us the strength and rest we need to endure and even overcome.

How are you sharing your husband's burdens today?

Tobi Henschel

Father, please give me the strength to help my husband bear his burdens. Help us both to remember to lean on You to carry these burdens, and not depend on our own strength. Amen.

Fishbowl Living—Accepting and Forgetting   4

But with me it is a very small thing that I should be judged by you or by any human court. In fact, I do not even judge myself. For I am not aware of anything against myself, but I am not thereby acquitted. It is the Lord who judges me.

1 Corinthians 4:3-4

The house we lived in during our first small-town ministry was "backwards." The back wall of our chalet-style house was patterned with many large windows placed to view the tree-covered ravine from the living area. This design placed the bedrooms at the front of the house, meaning the bedroom windows were the ones that faced the road, one of the main highways that laced through the town.

A lot of cars passed our house, and, as is common in rural areas, people who knew us would honk to be friendly as they sped by. One Sunday, a few years after we'd moved to this town, my husband informed me that someone had asked him why we kept our blinds closed.

I'm not really sure what I said, but I probably went on a big tirade about how it was none of that person's business whether or not our blinds were closed!

Fishbowl living as a pastor and wife has its downside all right, but having people watch you is part of being in leadership. How can I come to terms with being the one in the fishbowl? I need to remember to overlook the offenses and accept my leadership position; some things aren't worth getting angry over (Proverbs 19:11). Second, I can consider that others are not the judge of my decisions. Paul said, "It is the Lord who judges me" (1 Corinthians 4:4).

Finally, when I am tempted to fear what others think, I recall that "The fear of man lays a snare, but whoever trusts in the LORD is safe" (Proverbs 29:25).

I will never please everyone, and if I try, I am the one who is ensnared. I want to fear God, not man. Then I can close my blinds or leave them open. I can pray that those looking in will see that the fish swimming in this bowl are creatures who are seeking to glorify God that others might be pointed to Him.

Wendy McCready

God, let me fear You first. Let me be gracious to others, loving them as You would but finding peace in knowing that You are the one Who judges me. Let me listen to Your voice above the voices of others. Amen.

Come to me, all who labor and are heavy laden, and I will give you rest. Take my yoke upon you, and learn from me, for I am gentle and lowly in heart, and you will find rest for your souls. For my yoke is easy, and my burden is light.

Matthew 11:28-30

*Y*ou will never serve God more than He is serving you.

You are doing a great many things; of this I have no doubt. You may be going through a dark season of much service and sacrifice and not have much to show for it. But this I know — God's service to you always surpasses your service for Him. The problem comes when our gaze is heavy on our own service and what is being asked of us, and we lose sight of the fact that we are being served by a God who got down on His knees to wash the feet of His followers (John 13:1-20).

Today Jesus doesn't just ask of you — He kneels down in front of you. And yet how many times have I kicked over His washbasin in my clumsy rush to do all the things I feel the press of? And then flopped down at the end of the day declaring how drained and empty I am? And I wonder — how does the gentle, serving Father take my dramatic display? With grace, undoubtedly, because always, His service remains.

I cannot number for you all the ways I am served by the One I am supposed to be serving, so I will linger simply on this — I never serve alone.

What greater comfort and strength is there than knowing that Jesus is here *now*? Right now in, yes — *even this*. All the complexities and weighty burdens and ministry (and family) can feel crushing. And they are! When I was a very young pastor's wife and having a baby every couple of years, it used to confound me that Jesus declared, "My yoke is easy and my burden is light."

What was wrong with me, that this felt neither easy nor light? Ah, but this secret I have learned--it isn't easy; it isn't light. It's that He is just so strong and just so present, such "a very present help in trouble" (Psalm 46:1), that I am free to move, yes *even to run* under His yoke because ultimately, He has placed the burden on His own shoulders instead of on my own.

Sarah Johnson

Lord, help me today to see Your kneeling service to me, and may my own serving be transformed. Amen.

A Waterfall of God's Grace: 6
Healing for Sexual Harassment

Deep calls to deep at the roar of your waterfalls; all your breakers and your waves have gone over me. By day the LORD commands his steadfast love, and at night his song is with me, a prayer to the God of my life.

Psalm 42:7-8

Listening to a waterfall's rhythmical echoes of time and space leaves me satisfied. The musical language of waterfalls must have started in Paradise with Eve attending the continual symphony of cascading blues and silver.

Waterfalls are rare in the Sandhills of north-central Nebraska where I live. The water is underground, brought up by windmills to water the cattle and grasslands. Similarly, the windmill of God's grace has been bringing up life-giving water in my life.

I lived my middle-school years as a shy, quiet girl. Unwanted attention came my way, and I was sexually harassed by a male teacher repeatedly for three years. A cork of fear kept my voice bottled inside.

Those awkward and embarrassing years were still affecting me years later while I was a pastor's wife living in an isolated context. I found myself unable to speak truth or to share a personal testimony of God's goodness.

I met one-on-one with an older lady who travels to counsel trainees. She listened and then told my story back to me in third person. We went to prayer, asking Jesus to heal my pain. I felt my voice being uncorked, and a song cascaded forth, "I love You, Lord, and I lift my voice, to worship You."

This shy gal was ready to praise the Healer, and new courage started flowing. My first waterfall moment came when I shared my testimony with our dear church family. The night before, I wasn't sure I could actually follow through and share this part of my story, but God's grace was surely enough. And my moment of transparency led to other women sharing parts of their story with me. Waterfalls of grace feed other waterfalls.

As a girl, I would pick out a single drop of water at the top of a waterfall and keep my eye on it until it landed in the refreshing coolness below. Just as fresh water continues to cycle over a waterfall, the waterfall of His grace is always running fresh in our lives.

Denna Busenitz

Jesus, let me be like that one drop of water as I fall continually into Your refreshing and healing grace. Awaken new areas of courage and stir my heart ever towards forgiveness. Amen.

Note: If you are currently in a situation where you are experiencing abuse or have experienced such in the past, be sure to seek counsel regarding reporting that abuse as well as receive counseling to aid in healing.

Let us then with confidence draw near to the throne of grace, that we may receive mercy and find grace to help in time of need.
                                                            Hebrews 4:16

$\mathcal{P}$raying.

How can one little word bring comfort? Peacc? Encouragement?

I've gone through some major health battles the past couple years, and I believe that the prayers of my friends and family, including my church family, helped me to stay calm and joyful in the battles.

When Jesus was on earth, He healed people with a word, a touch, a mixture of mud and spit. One group of men wanted so much for their friend to be healed that they disassembled a roof to lower their friend in front of Jesus.

There are times that I picture my prayers in the same way. I am picking up my friend and laying her at the feet of Jesus, asking Him to heal her. He hears our prayers, and He works in lives to heal, to strengthen, to give wisdom, to bless as He wills. It is good to have prayers surrounding you every day, but especially when the way is hard.

Knowing that people are carrying you to the Throne of Grace is a great encouragement, and it keeps you focused on the glorious fact that God is in control, that you are not alone, and that you are loved.

I've found that sharing my burdens, my current circumstances, and my needs with others allows them to share my burdens, pray for wisdom in my circumstances, and even provide for my needs.

Hearing that people are praying for me lifts my heart and eases my burden. I'm thankful when they tell me they are praying.

This is a reminder to you today. There are many people in our lives who are dealing with stress, illness, financial struggles, depression, heartbreak, or rebellious children. Whether the problems are small or large, people need our prayers to continue to be faithful, to be strong in the midst of their storms, and to be assured of God's faithfulness. Spend time in prayer for them, and then, let them know that you have carried them to the Throne of Grace.

Lynnette Goebel

Heavenly Father, thank You for the precious gift of prayer. Thank You for Jesus Who opened the way for us to enter into Your Presence through prayer. Help us to never take You for granted. Remind me, Father, to pray for people who need Your Presence in their lives, who need Your healing power, and who need Your strength and peace. We praise You for your lovingkindness to us. Amen.

Therefore I tell you, do not be anxious about your life, what you will eat or what you will drink, nor about your body, what you will put on. Is not life more than food, and the body more than clothing?
Matthew 6:25

*W*e are rarely given the sweet gift of seeing exactly what God is up to. So many times, I wonder how this day fits into God's great plan of redemption for the world. I often wonder if my little life makes a difference. I always feel like I could be "doing" more. But almost in that same moment, I feel that gentle whisper of the Lord say, "I don't need you to be so busy 'doing' that you miss 'being,'" and I'm reminded to simply abide in the love of my heavenly Father who lavishes His love on me (1 John 3:1).

We have to preach the gospel to ourselves daily; otherwise, we get caught up in a works-based, grace-deprived lifestyle of trying to be enough. I'm not enough. That's the point. The gospel says I was dead, and Jesus resurrected my lifeless soul to new life with Him. He made a trade, an unfair deal. He took my sin, and I got eternal life. I bring nothing to the table, and He brings everything. But He gives grace upon grace to empower me to live a godly life (2 Peter 1:3).

This life is about more than having our temporal needs met. If how we spend our time and money reveals what we really treasure, then my day would reveal that I treasure many things that are temporary. If I can shift from thinking that daily tasks have only temporal worth to realizing that they have eternal value, then I can turn every activity into worship.

Worship is an eternal offering, storing up treasure in heaven (Matthew 6:20). I stay busy with caring for four children, doing dishes and laundry, running errands, etc. But if each time I do those simple tasks, I go deeper into those secret ministries mentioned earlier in Matthew 6 (vv. 4, 6, 18), then I have just gained treasure in Heaven.

A slight shift of perspective can give your daily business eternal worth! Seek His face, and He will surely meet your needs!

Chelsea Hall

Lord, I worship You for who You are, not for what You can do for me. And I give you my days, not for what I can do for You each day, but my life and my love as an offering. Amen.

Putting Others First 9

Let each of you look not only to his own interests, but also to the interests of others.

Philippians 2:4

When my 6-year-old son chose to attend a classmate's birthday party at a splash pad, I was pleasantly surprised as he isn't a big fan of water, especially when it gets in his face. I was amused when he showed me what he wrote in his friend's birthday card, "I don't really like water, but I do like you."

That simple sentence has been rattling around in my brain for some time, along with the words from Philippians 2:4: "Let each of you look not only to his own interests, but also to the interests of others." This verse comes right in the middle of Paul's beautiful depiction of what it means to be like Christ, along with phrases like "having the same love" (2:2) and "count others more significant than yourselves" (2:3).

Once I stopped chuckling at my son's brutal but sweet honesty, I was challenged by his simple action of putting his friend's interests before his own, although I'm sure the hope of birthday cake made his sacrifice a little easier. How often do I fail to put the interests of others before my own? Am I willing to get a little water in my face if it means I can show love to others?

I often think that in order to show love to the people around me, the deed has to be big in order to be noticeable. After all, Christ's dying on the cross was *big*, and that's the ultimate showing of love, right? But I forget that in order to get to the cross, Jesus had to humble Himself (2:8).

Humble myself and put others first—these are the ways I need to show love to others. It doesn't need to be big and showy. As I take on the mind of Christ, He will show me the simple ways I can show love to those around me, even if that means getting a little water in my face.

What way can you "get a little water in your face" today? How can you put others first today?

Tobi Henschel

Lord, give me humility that I might put others first. Help me to see the ways that I can honor them and show them love, even if the ways seem small. Amen.

I give thanks to my God always for you because of the grace of God that was given you in Christ Jesus.

1 Corinthians 1:4

"Sometimes I want to hide in the bathroom," a friend once said to me, confessing her struggle to love a certain individual in the church. Does that sound slightly familiar? The opinions, sins, and personality types within the church can really start to irritate us. We might not actually hide in the bathroom, but we're annoyed all the same.

As tempting as it is to duck out of class due to personality conflicts, that's not the way of Christ. Have you noticed how Paul begins his letters in the New Testament? Within the first several paragraphs, he basically shouts, "I'm thankful!" And his thankfulness is always specific. He's thankful, continuously, for the specific church to which he's writing.

Sometimes Paul's thankfulness makes sense. For instance, the Ephesian believers were known for their faith in Christ and their love for God's people (Ephesians 1:15). Of course, Paul was thankful for them!

Paul's thankfulness for the Corinthian church, however, is baffling. This was a church plagued by problems, including division and immorality. Paul knew that some people in the church didn't like him, yet before he addresses the many issues in this community, Paul starts his letter by saying, "I give thanks to my God always for you because of the grace of God that was given you in Christ Jesus" (1 Corinthians 1:4).

Paul thanked God for this flawed church because his eyes were fixed on the saving work of Christ. The cross filled his vision, and, where we would expect to see hands thrown up in exasperation, we find, incomprehensibly, thanksgiving instead. This is the power of the cross.

People disappoint us. That's reality. I'm pretty sure my flaws exasperate team members at times, and your personality might annoy someone across the aisle. How could such petty humanity ever result in God-glorifying unity? The answer is, and could only be, Jesus.

Are there church members whom you find hard to love? Look at the cross. Thank God for the vast love He has lavished on them.

We fight Satan's schemes for disunity by proclaiming thankfulness for Christ's redemptive work. His work within His people is good and glorious and worthy of praise!

Amber Beery

Father, through the power of Your Spirit, produce an abundance of gentleness, love, kindness, peace, patience, self-control, faithfulness, and goodness within my church family so that we will reflect You more and more every day to each other and to the watching world. Thank You for the love and grace You have lavished on us. Amen.

Hospitality in the Home   11

Show hospitality to one another without grumbling. As each has received a gift, use it to serve one another, as good stewards of God's varied grace... in order that in everything God may be glorified through Jesus Christ. To him belong glory and dominion forever and ever. Amen.

1 Peter 4:9-11

I love visiting and laughing with friends over food. Once the whirlwind of house cleaning, preparing, and cooking subsides, I realize the satisfaction of hosting church family. Sometimes we talk about God and our Christian walks. Other times more down-to-earth subjects like kids and vacations come up. Hospitality also provides opportunities for my growth and refinement.

When we invite people over, my husband and I strategize topics of conversation or questions we can ask. We find brainstorming helps us focus the conversation on our guests instead of ourselves. After one particular visit, we discovered we missed asking a crucial question.

A couple and their two little children were among the last young families with whom we had yet to connect one-on-one since we arrived two years earlier. We had them over for lunch and learned a lot about them that Sunday.

They are quieter people, but our time together felt successful after a good meal, chatting about parenting, and reminiscing about our wedding days. The conversation was mostly light-hearted small talk, but it was still very enjoyable and genuine.

A few days later we were shaken to read a prayer email with news that the young dad's test for cancer had come back positive. My stomach turned when we found out they had heavy news on their hearts. I wish they had felt free to bring it up. We also could have given them a more direct opportunity! All I know is that we did not ask, "How can we pray for you?"

Praying with dinner guests is a "pastor thing," but that is not a reason to shy away from it. Our motivation to pray for others should be that we care for them. Caring for people moves us from entertaining to hospitality. Remember that hosting is never about perfect food or polished counters. None of our self-focused thoughts really matter when we stop to pray with others.

Our questions may give opportunity for important topics to surface, even if we think we know about everything in our small-town churches and communities. That night we decided we would always stop and pray with our guests. Praying is always worth it. It is one more opportunity for God to be glorified in our hospitality.

Nicole Martin

As we love those we have in our home, Lord, give us humility and courage to bring requests before Your holy throne. In Jesus' name, Amen.

But when he saw the wind, he was afraid, and beginning to sink he cried out, "Lord, save me." Jesus immediately reached out his hand and took hold of him, saying to him, "O you of little faith, why did you doubt?"

Matthew 14:30-31

I mess up a lot. I say things I regret; I regularly forget to look to God for my strength; and nothing seems to go the way that I had planned. Life can get really mixed up sometimes.

Matthew 14:24-33 illustrates why it is so important to cry out to Jesus when we start to sink beneath the weight of our imperfection. Can you imagine? It was early morning, perhaps still quite dark, and the disciples had spent a rough night battling the wind and waves while Jesus prayed alone on a mountain. Suddenly someone looked up and saw Jesus walking toward them over the waves. The disciples were afraid.

Peter wanted to prove it really was Jesus, and he said, "Lord, if it is You, command me to come to You on the water" (v. 28).

Have you ever felt like God was calling you to do something that you were sure you were incapable of doing?

Peter stepped out on the water. One step, two steps, three steps… he's doing it, he's walking on the water, but it's really windy and he's starting to look around at the waves surrounding him. He's not focusing on Jesus, who is reaching out to him across the waves. Suddenly the sea water is up to his ankles, his knees, then his waist.

Peter knew he was sinking. Matthew 14:30 tells us that Peter cried out to be saved, and immediately Jesus reached out His hand and lifted Peter up. He didn't put Peter back in the boat, but He drew Peter to Himself on the angry sea. He pulled Peter to Himself and kept him safe in the midst of the storm. Together they went back to the safety of the boat, with Peter held securely in Jesus' arms.

Jesus reaches out to us in the midst of our imperfection because we are His children and He loves us. We will always come up short when we rely on ourselves. Jesus has redeemed us through the shedding of His blood, and every time we call out to Him in our imperfection, we experience that redemption through His faithfulness to us.

Marcy Ardis

Dear Lord, help me to remember to call out to You when my path seems unclear. Guide me safely through the turmoil that surrounds me. Thank You for being here for me, even when I turn away and forget to focus only on You. Amen.

The end of all things is at hand; therefore be self-controlled and sober-minded for the sake of your prayers. Above all, keep loving one another earnestly, since love covers a multitude of sins.

1 Peter 4:7-8

*I*t hits me when I stand next to a daughter who's almost taller than I am or when I glance across the table and see a hint of a man's expression on the boy-child's face.

Time's short. Love well. That simple reminder is at the heart of Peter's message in these verses.

Do you hear the ticking of the clock? Time's short. Jesus is coming. Following Christ means living with expectation as we anticipate the day Christ pulls back the veil of eternity and returns for His own. In these last fleeting moments of human history, Peter charges us to love well.

In his commentary on 1 Peter 1, Howard Marshall writes that the Greek expression for *loving each other earnestly* means "to love at full stretch." This is not a passive kind of love. Love requires work, growth, and vulnerability. It demands that we work through conflicts, live with differences, and find ways to love people who aren't like we are.

Peter wrote this letter to a persecuted and alienated church that needed a safe harbor in a hostile world. As they anticipated Christ's return, they needed to dedicate themselves to loving well, building relationships that would sustain the inevitable frictions of life together. Love binds the church together so we don't fracture apart.

Like the churches to which Peter first wrote, we live in a world that is not always friendly to our faith. Loving well helps us to take advantage of every moment—showing grace to one another and inviting the lost to come home. Christ is coming, and too many are still unprepared. Our time is too precious to waste.

Time's short. Love well.

Leigh Powers

Lord, I look forward to the day You return. As I anticipate Your coming, help me to make use of the time You have given me. Show me what it means to love well. Amen.

Therefore encourage one another and build one another up, just as you are doing.

1 Thessalonians 5:11

$\mathcal{D}$r. Erwin W. Lutzer is pastor emeritus of The Moody Church where he served as the senior pastor for 36 years. He is also an award-winning author of numerous books.

In his autobiography, *He Will Be the Preacher,* he wrote about people who came alongside his family early in their ministry. One couple had them over for dinner, stocked their fridge with food, and drew them into their family. An older couple "took us under their wing and treated us as if we were their own children. ...These families were models to us of kindness and generosity" (page 171).

These families were ordinary people who made an impact on their pastor and his family. And many years later, that now rather famous pastor remembered their kindnesses and wrote about them in his book.

Sadly, many pastors have an abundance of negative stories about which to write—an example of what not to do. I hope they also have some wonderful stories as well.

It is exciting to think that we in the church can be a part of God's plan in the lives of our pastor and his family by simply being an encouragement to them.

It is frightening to think that we can grieve the Holy Spirit and discourage our pastor and his wife by the way we treat them. It is hard to realize that some people have left their ministries because of how they have been treated.

Years ago, after some struggles within my church, I decided that I wanted to be the kind of person whom people will miss when I'm gone. I don't want them to be happy that I am no longer there causing trouble.

Lynnette Goebel

Heavenly Father, I pray that today You will prompt people to encourage their pastors and their pastors' families. I ask that ordinary people in ordinary churches would see the impact they can have on the lives of their pastors — to realize that You sent that pastor to them as their shepherd. May they feel grateful for these men and their families. Encourage Your under-shepherds and keep them strong as they serve You among the sheep of Your hand. Amen.

A Pastor's Wife's Cheer: Part One

When the cares of my heart are many, your consolations cheer my soul.

Psalm 94:19

*A*s the wife of a rural church-planting pastor, I note one similar task between the cheerleaders I knew in high school and me — to unify the crowd (congregation) with effective cheers for the team (pastor).

Join me as I lead my first pastor's wife **CHEER!** Count it a joy to serve together; **H**ear his heart; **B**e Elastic; **E**ncourage; **R**econcile quickly.

Count it a joy to serve together. Aquila and Priscilla give an effective example of a couple serving well. In Romans 16:4b, Paul says of them, "I give thanks, but all the churches of the Gentiles give thanks as well." The blessing of a couple who enjoys serving together has the potential of a louder and longer reverberation.

Consider your team strengths as you serve together: shepherding; planning; discipling; evangelizing; counseling; visiting; family time...

Hear his heart. My husband and I take a few minutes in the morning to connect, asking: What is the one thing you need most from me? What are you looking forward to? Not looking forward to? How can I pray for you?

We've started a nightly routine: What was the best part of your day? The hardest part? Did you sense my encouragement? How did God's grace show up? Let's give our cheering voices a rest and listen daily to our husbands' heart.

Be Elastic. I prefer plan A, but we often need to go with plans B-Z, don't we? I once emptied four kitchen cupboards' worth of items when there was a knock at the door. What's a pastor's wife to do?! I invited the church lady in, and we had a great visit right in the midst of my piles. I pray for wisdom (and flexibility!) every time I hear a knock at the door or the phone rings. The best stretch routine I know is to pray throughout my day.

My husband helps me adjust to new things and I help him appreciate routine. I imagine Priscilla cheering Aquila on as they served Christ together.

Denna Busenitz

Jesus, I ask for Your help as I cheer my husband on. I count it a joy to serve together. Help me to listen to his heart. Enable me to be flexible when needed as I pray my way through each day. Amen.

An excellent wife who can find? She is far more precious than jewels. The heart of her husband trusts in her, and he will have no lack of gain. She does him good, and not harm, all the days of her life.
                                                                Proverbs 31:10-12

Remember our pastor's wife **CHEER**? Count it a joy to serve together; Hear his heart; Be Elastic; Encourage; Reconcile quickly.

Today, we look at **Encourage**. Here's my top-3 list as I've asked other PWs:
1. Love him instead of correct him.
2. Be patient with him.
3. Share with him how his ministry/sermons bless you.

Lois Seadore has served as a small-town pastor's wife for over forty years. She says, "We don't need to tell him every negative thing we hear or even think about people. Let's protect our husband from having to control his thoughts and attitude as he works to love and guide the sheep."

A "Cheer" Poem from a Pastor to His Wife
by Pastor Kurt Busenitz

Faithful to his wife and God —
This harmony should not be odd.
But ministry can take its toll,
And put a strain on heart and soul.
What can she do in times like these?
She calms her heart on bended knees.
To cheer him on is to be her calling —
Stand beside him and keep from falling.

Celebrate, be flexible, and hear his heart—
She must not lose sight of her crucial part.
A heart endeared is a powerful glue—
Reconcile often for a love that's true.

A "Cheer" Poem from a PW to Her Husband
by Denna Busenitz

Preach, teach—shepherd the sheep.
Baptize, counsel, and wisely give reasons.
Laugh with our kids—commune with God deep.
Love your wife through all the seasons.
Make disciples, lead and guide—
Treasure your cheerleader by your side.
Plow, sow, and harvest well—
Of God's goodness to others tell.

Denna Busenitz

Lord God, let me be an encouragement to my husband. Together may we flee to You for refuge and strong encouragement as we hold fast to the hope set before us. Amen.
(from Hebrews 6:18)

A Pastor's Wife's Cheer: Part Three

17

That their hearts may be encouraged, being knit together in love, to reach all the riches of full assurance of understanding and the knowledge of God's mystery, which is Christ.

Colossians 2:2

*T*ime for the last part in our Pastor's Wife's **CHEER** — Count it a joy to serve together; Hear his heart; Be Elastic; Encourage; Reconcile quickly.

Reconcile quickly. A PW once told her husband on their wedding night she would never hide anything from him save one thing, the contents of a box she would keep under their bed. After 20 years, her husband finally asked what was in the box. She reluctantly told him, "Two eggs and $1000. You see, every time you preached a good sermon, I put in $1." The pastor smiled and asked, "What about the two eggs?" She admitted, "I put one egg in every time you preached a bad sermon." He exclaimed, "Well, that's pretty good for 20 years of sermons!" She swallowed hard and said, "Yes, but every time I got a dozen eggs, I sold them."

Do you and I have a hidden box of hurtful words or thoughts against our husband? As PWs, it's our privilege to keep short accounts with our shepherd-husbands as they prepare to weekly shepherd the flock.

Four Steps of Forgiveness (adapted from <u>Caring for the Heart Ministries</u>)
1. Release the person who has hurt us — the first and possibly hardest step.

2. Open wide the wallet of our heart and pay for the hurt others caused. God budgets big grace not only to us personally, but also to help us forgive others.

3. Let Jesus heal the damage done to our heart; He's an expert healer and knows down to the last drop what kind of healing balm we need. "He heals the brokenhearted" (Psalm 147:3a).

4. Ask Jesus, "What do You want me to do with the pain in my heart that resulted from the hurt?" Four things happen almost simultaneously in this fourth and final step of forgiveness. We give our pain to Jesus, let Him take it, let Jesus' healing in, and let the pain out. Our Creator God wired us to experience forgiveness, and it's life-giving!

Denna Busenitz

I pray that the God of endurance and encouragement would help my husband and me to live in such harmony with one another, in accord with Christ Jesus, that together we would with one voice glorify the God and Father of our Lord Jesus Christ. Amen. *(from Romans 15:5-6)*

Have this mind among yourselves, which is yours in Christ Jesus, who, though he was in the form of God, did not count equality with God a thing to be grasped, but made himself nothing, taking the form of a servant, being born in the likeness of men.

Philippians 2:5-7

*E*very pastor's wife has one. It's on a shelf, tucked away in a den somewhere. It's tacked on a hallway wall space where not too many guests walk by, or it's folded away in a drawer ready to come out once a year for the Christmas season.

It's that gift that someone from the congregation has given you that you aren't quite sure what it is or how to use it...or you really just think it's ugly, but you don't want to offend her by not having it up somewhere!

My grandmother was a pastor's wife for many years, and she always told me that if I don't receive what people give to me, I am keeping them from receiving a blessing from God for giving.

Those are wise words, but I haven't always been so good about receiving from my guests. For a lot of years, I thought that hospitality was primarily about giving to others — putting out fancy food on my grandmother's china on the table bedecked with fresh flowers and handwritten place cards for each guest.

Of course it's fine to be hospitable in this way, but I often found when I was in the middle of harried preparations for the next Sunday dinner after church or snacks for home Bible study and I didn't have time to vacuum, the Holy Spirit would whisper to me, "Wendy, Wendy, you are worried and upset over many things. Choose what Mary chose" (Luke 10:38-42).

I have learned from others who have hosted me in their homes over the years that I have felt most comfortable in places where I was treated like one of the family.

Sometimes we just need to swallow our pride and serve a peanut butter and jelly sandwich to a hungry college-aged young man because our spaghetti has run out.

In these small and yet significant ways, we can minister God's grace to others in our homes, even with that mystery item displayed on the shelf. Maybe it will just become a conversation piece you can use to make the next person who walks through your doors feel like she is coming home.

Wendy McCready

Lord, help me to remember that what is most important is my heart in serving You and others. May others be blessed as they come into my home, whether I am giving or receiving. Amen.

When My Husband Is Criticized: **19**
Part One

For we do not wrestle against flesh and blood, but against the rulers, against the authorities, against the cosmic powers over this present darkness, against the spiritual forces of evil in the heavenly places.
Ephesians 6:12

Sometimes I think that being married to a pastor is like being married to a boxer — you aren't directly getting hit, but every time your husband gets "hit" (criticized), you feel it, too.

While pastors need to be held accountable, it often feels as if this turns into unrealistic expectations for them. Never sin. Never mess up. Never hurt someone's feelings. In short, don't be human. But my husband is human, and he does mess up. Therefore, he will face heavy criticism — some just and some unjust. How should I respond when this happens?

I want to respond as if I'm in the ring opposite these people, ready to strike back at them. I want to rage against the responsible parties, to rally my troops and stage a defense. I want to bring in champions who will squash the opposition.

As soon as I slow down enough to take a breath and listen, the Holy Spirit whispers to me, "Against whom is your battle?" As my heart begins to soften, I remember the words of Ephesians 6:12. My brothers and sisters in Christ are not the enemy. Satan is.

Satan would love for us to tear apart the body of Christ from the inside out. We are in an intense spiritual battle, and criticism (well-intentioned or not) can often be a tool of his to cause great damage.

However, criticism can also be a great tool in God's hands to stretch, strengthen, and grow each of us. If we are never stretched, we will never grow. If we are never challenged, we will stagnate.

So how should we respond to criticism? We must root our response in love, the starting point of reconciliation. We love because He first loved us (1 John 4:19). We must respond with love, whether we are in the wrong or not. We must let Christ's love flow through us and be the artist's brush that paints every word or action of our response.

How are you currently responding to the criticism you and your husband face?

Tobi Henschel

Father, help me to learn and grow from criticism as You intend. Give me wisdom and patience to endure, and Your love to respond to those who hurt us. Amen.

When My Husband Is Criticized: *20*
Part Two

Do not repay evil for evil or reviling for reviling, but on the contrary, bless, for to this you were called, that you may obtain a blessing.

1 Peter 3:9

*W*hen our husbands are being criticized, it is easy to respond in anger or with retaliation. Instead, we need to respond by blessing others. Here are seven ways to respond to criticism in love:

1. Listen Respectfully
Listen to the criticism without immediately becoming defensive. Listen and promise to pray about what they've said. This opens the door for reconciliation and growth.

2. Pray
Seek God's leading. Ask Him to reveal any areas of sin or wrongdoing on your part. Pray also for those who are criticizing you. Thank God for them, pray blessings on them, pray that God would lead them, and pray for God to give you His love for them.

3. Seek Godly Advice
Go to the leaders in your church and humbly seek their advice. Work together to build a plan for responding to this situation Biblically. Ask for a mediator to be present at the next conversation to help bring a more objective perspective to the table.

4. Remember That Hurt People, Hurt People
When people hurt us, it helps to remember they may be hurting as well, and it is a reminder to pray for them in their own hurts.

Also, ask God for patience and love towards those around you, to help you to not take out your hurt on them.

5. Cry Out to God in Grief

Criticism hurts. Take time to pour out your heart to God in grief, and allow yourself time to hurt. You may not need to cry literal tears like I do, but we all need to cry out to God for His healing.

6. Get Some Distance

Take time to get away and to stop thinking about the criticism. A vacation, a family day, an evening away with your husband, or a different area of ministry—find a way to gain distance because with distance comes perspective.

7. Be Encouraged by the Good

Look around for the ways God has blessed or encouraged you recently: a kind word from someone at church, a hug, a sweet card, a financial gift, or a dear church member who serves faithfully. Also, look around you for ways to be a blessing to others. Focusing on God's blessings to us and being His blessing to others can bring healing.

In which of these ways can you grow for your response to criticism?

Tobi Henschel

Lord, please help me to see how I can turn my hurts into blessings in the lives of those around me. Give me Your healing and Your love for others. Amen.

Blessed be the God and Father of our Lord Jesus Christ, the Father of mercies and God of all comfort, who comforts us in all our affliction, so that we may be able to comfort those who are in any affliction, with the comfort with which we ourselves are comforted by God. For as we share abundantly in Christ's sufferings, so through Christ we share abundantly in comfort too.

2 Corinthians 1:3-5

Rarely, a commercial will catch my attention and bring a tear to my eye. One Christmas season offered one of those moments for me.

A farm girl races home every day from the school bus stop to hand-stitch something in her room. Mom watches each day, but the girl does not share her task with Mom. After weeks of the same routine, when the girl races home from school, she sees her dad, shearing her sheep of a thick coat of wool. She runs into the house and comes back with her hand-stitched blanket, covering the sheep who no longer has a warm coat.

"Christmas is what you make it."

I didn't see the ad often, but it stayed in my mind all season. It made me think.

The child knew the shearing was coming, and her love for the animal made her prepare for the inevitable. She used the skills and time she had to provide warmth when it was needed.

Isn't this what our daily walk with the Lord should be—our learning and using our skills and time to prepare for when we see people in need?

I love sheep. I love the picture of Jesus as the Good Shepherd caring for us—His often-wayward sheep. A picture of sheep grazing on a green hillside shows tranquility and peace, and I wish I could step into the picture and rest. Psalm 23 often rescues my soul from the busyness and anxiety of life.

This commercial made me consider how I can bring comfort to others in the fold. When I was little, my mom called the big fluffy blanket on my bed a comforter. In the winter, I loved to snuggle down under that warm and cozy blanket (I still do.). My thoughts now ask how I can be a comforter to others.

Lynnette Goebel

Father, teach me new skills that You can use to help others. Prepare me. Lord, open my eyes to see others who have needs: physical needs, emotional needs, spiritual needs. Give me love for each person. Whisper to me how You want to use me to give them comfort. Use me.

Heavenly Father, give me compassion to give to others because of Your great mercy and grace which You have shown to me. Amen.

Your word is a lamp to my feet and a light to my path.
                                            Psalm 119:105

Soaring melodies. Pulsing rhythms. The Pandora Gladiator station pounds epic movie scores through the seams of the garage, and I half expect to see heroic acts of valor when I push open the door.

Instead, I'm greeted by everyday life. A car with its hood propped open. Spark plugs. My husband leaning into the engine of his sister's car. It's ordinary at first glance, but a second look, prompted by the epic music, reveals a display of the glory of God's kingdom — kindness in a garage, late on a Friday night, when the weekend calls.

Sometimes I wish a soundtrack could follow us all day long. Imagine if soaring music broke in at the kitchen table, prompting words of kindness instead of impatience. Imagine if suspenseful dissonance warned, "That's gossip. Stop talking." Imagine if an allegro composition reminded us to serve, unseen, with joy.

Imagination aside, we have something better than a soundtrack. We have words. Beautiful, inspiring, life-giving, truth-telling words from God.

The psalmist in Psalm 119 vividly shows us a life lived to the soundtrack of God's Word. He says, "Your decrees are the theme of my song wherever I lodge" (Psalm 119:54 NIV). He declares that God's words are our life's light, guiding our path (v. 105). They strengthen us in sorrow and give hope and comfort in suffering (vv. 28, 49-50). God's words reveal that His children are clothed in kindness (Colossians 3:12), that patience is the fruit of following the Merciful One (Galatians 5:22), and that humility is the way of the King (Philippians 2:1-11). They reveal the Word whose light is the life of humanity (John 1:1-5).

What a gift to have God's words fill and transform all the ordinary days of our lives wherever each moment takes us — the kitchen table, a business trip, the church nursery, etc. A heart and mind overflowing with the words of our faithful God is a delight worth time and effort!

So turn up the soundtrack! Listen to — learn — the words of our Shepherd and embrace the joy of life lived to the rhythm of His truth and in relationship with Him.

Amber Beery

Father, how I love Your words! They are the joy of my heart and bring light to my life. Yet I am prone to wander in the desert instead of being planted by the streams of life and dwelling in Your truth. Help me not to neglect Your Word. Amen.

Submit yourselves therefore to God. Resist the devil, and he will flee from you. Draw near to God, and he will draw near to you.

James 4:7-8a

*T*he first thing I noticed when I stepped out my front door was the sweet-and-sour scent of freshly mown hay. Our farmer neighbor was turning over the crop to ready it for baling and stacking and storing; it was the scent of early summer.

Life as a rural and small-town pastor's wife affords many opportunities to see God's truths displayed in the seasons. Our spiritual life also has different seasons of growth as we become conformed to Christ.

So, how do we cultivate our spiritual life no matter what season we are in?

I think the key to growth in our spiritual life is not necessarily (gasp!) reading our Bible for longer periods or praying more or fasting more. We certainly need a steady diet of the Word and prayer if we are going to grow, but I have come to learn over the years that I grow in my walk with Christ most when I embrace the season in which God has placed me and submit to God's will in it. I can know the Bible well and miss spiritual growth if I don't believe and obey what I read in it.

As women we are well familiar with seasons of life: the single years, the honeymoon stage of early married life, the joy of holding our firstborn.

But these seasons come with heartache, too – loneliness, disappointing relationships, miscarriage, or just the feeling of being stuck at home with endless nights of interrupted sleep and endless days of diapers and nose wiping. It goes on, and we wonder, how is any of this spiritual? I can't even get a minute to myself to have quiet and peace unless I'm in the washroom!

Embrace your current season, dear fellow pastor's wife. Whatever season we are in, we need to submit to God's will in it.

Just as the farmer submits to the laws of the land in order to receive the growth of his crop, so we will cultivate a spiritual life when we submit to the season in which we find ourselves, trusting in our Good Father, the Cultivator of all spiritual fruit.

Wendy McCready

Lord, I confess that submission is hard, but the more I do it, the easier it will become. Give me the grace to obey You where I am struggling to listen today. Amen.

If we live by the Spirit, let us also walk by the Spirit.

Galatians 5:25

I have struggled over the years with so much guilt in cultivating a spiritual life because many of the tools I was given were legalistic lists of things to do but to which I could never measure up. Over the years I have learned that, because I am dead, spiritual life isn't something I can make happen on my own; it's Christ's life, His Holy Spirit, in me that produces spiritual life.

Therefore, I can't count on the perfect time of day for my quiet time or the perfect number of minutes spent in prayer to help me grow spiritually. It's like how the seasons dictate for us when the soil is to be tilled, planted, and harvested. If I told you that I was going to plant corn in the fall and wait for it to come up in the spring, you'd think I was crazy (at least in North America). Yet we often submit our spiritual lives to our own timetables and formulas, expecting results and coming up fruitless.

It should be our desire to seek the Lord moment by moment, walking by the Spirit, submitting to whatever season we are in and whatever job we have in that season.

For example, during a potluck at our first church, I ended up across the table from a woman who was recently widowed. Her husband had struggled with mental challenges, and she was not known as the most gracious of women in our church. In fact, we knew she'd criticized my husband's ministry on a number of occasions in the past. But I knew I needed to reach out to her, to ask her how she was doing, to pour out the mercy and love of Christ to her.

I don't even remember what I said to her that day, but I know that God used me to bless her; I was totally energized in that moment, and she seemed softer towards me going forward. Not only that, my own attitude towards her had changed.

That is spiritual life, obeying God's Spirit in all things.

Seek the Lord and have life, women. If we embrace the season of life in which God has placed us and submit to and seek Him in it, then we will cultivate a spiritual life. Then we will reap the rewards of our labour in Him.

Wendy McCready

Lord, I want to walk by Your Spirit, seeking to learn of You no matter what season I find myself in right now. Teach me what You want to teach me and build Your life in me. Amen.

Let not steadfast love and faithfulness forsake you; bind them around your neck; write them on the tablet of your heart. So you will find favor and good success in the sight of God and man.
Proverbs 3:3-4

$\mathcal{A}$ few months ago, I decided that I needed to start dating again. This time I set my sights on dating my pastor. Of course, he's the same man I dated many years ago, but he has changed a lot, and so have I.

Proverbs 3:3-4 reminds me to be faithful and continually seek to love the man God has given me. This is not always an easy task as our days get filled with commitments and never-ending to-do lists. Choosing to date my husband is an intentional choice on my part to strengthen our marriage and the bond of love that we share.

My favourite date is going to the splash pad. We drive to our local town, buy a couple of coffees, and pull out the lawn chairs. While our daughter plays at the splash pad, we sit and talk about the things that interest us, the things that draw us together.

Another way we date each other is by spending some time in the early morning praying, reading the Bible, and talking about the upcoming day. We don't manage to do this every single day, but it is a wonderful way to start the day with the person I love before we each have to go our separate ways as the day progresses.

Last year my husband built a fire pit in our backyard. There is nothing nicer than being able to sit out with my husband and daughter, roasting marshmallows and gazing at the stars.

It is pretty romantic, even with our daughter joining us, because she is a part of who we are.

Another way I like to date my husband is late at night when we are driving in the car. We put on some music and we just talk. We talk about everything and anything, and, in doing so, we draw closer to one another. We have fun, we laugh, and we get to know each other all over again.

Talking is important, but all the talking in the world would be useless if we didn't listen to one another. Taking the time to really listen to what the other person is saying, and responding in meaningful ways helps us maintain a loving, healthy, and nurturing relationship.

Marcy Ardis

Dear Lord, thank You for my husband and the life You have given us. Help us to find the time to continue to purposely grow closer to one another. Help us also to be steadfast in the pursuit of growing in Your knowledge and wisdom as we study the Bible and pray together. Amen.

Dating Through the Seasons of Life 26

I therefore, a prisoner for the Lord, urge you to walk in a manner worthy of the calling to which you have been called, with all humility and gentleness, with patience, bearing with one another in love.
Ephesians 4:1-2

Recently, I have been focusing on the importance of mindfully spending quality time with my husband. The way we spend our time together now is very different from the way we spent time together when we were younger, but in some ways, it is much more meaningful. We understand how precious it is to have a few minutes together, and we value the time we have much more than we did in the past.

I find Ephesians 4:1-7 to be very convicting in terms of the way that I treat my husband. Am I being humble, gentle, patient, and loving in my interactions with him? When the day has been rough, and I start to get short-tempered, am I showing him the same grace that God has shown me? Can other people see this in our lives? Are we showing a good example of godly love to the people in our congregation and to our own child?

I have been thinking about how important it is to be faithful throughout all of our life's seasons. In our lives and in our marriages, we all face challenges that are unique to us and our families. Despite the personal nature of these challenges, we are all called to show the same faithfulness to our spouses.

When we have had a rough day, I have to ask myself whether I am acting as God would have me to act toward my husband. Together, are we exemplifying a godly marriage?

Do we serve each other in simple love when times get tough? Do we recognize the tiredness in each other and graciously serve one another, or are we pushing each other's buttons and making life worse? Are we willing to change how we spend time together, how we date one another, to meet the needs of our marriage as our lives unfold according to God's plan?

Our time is valuable, and there are often many things and people vying for it all at the same time. By choosing to purposely spend time together, we are choosing to be faithful to the person God has given to us.

Marcy Ardis

Dear Lord, help me to be a gentle person, walking in a way that is worthy of You. Stop me from taking my frustrations out on my husband. Allow me to faithfully show him a loving spirit every day. Amen.

Praying at all times in the Spirit, with all prayer and supplication.
To that end keep alert with all perseverance, making supplication
for all the saints, and also for me, that words may be given to me in
opening my mouth boldly to proclaim the mystery of the gospel, for
which I am an ambassador in chains, that I may declare it boldly,
as I ought to speak.

Ephesians 6:18-20

*L*iving in a house with three small boys means I'm sur-
rounded by a lot of superhero paraphernalia, and I often hear
statements like, "I can shoot ice from my hands," or "My superpower is the best superpower!"

Sometimes I wish I had superpowers to help my husband
with his endless pastoral workload, that I could finish all of
his administrative tasks in a few seconds and give him supernatural boosts of energy to make it through.

The reality is I already have the best superpower for helping
my husband — prayer! I can bring anything and everything
before our great and almighty God Who holds everything in
His hands.

The apostle Paul asked the Ephesian church to pray for him.
He needed the prayer support of his church family to do what
God called him to do in his ministry, just as my husband
needs my prayer support to do his job.
We spend precious times of prayer together over church matters, and God uses those times to knit us closer together as a
couple and as His servants. It grows our love for each other
and for our shared ministry. It brings us peace in the midst of
uncertainty and courage to face the unknown.

At times when I don't know what to pray, I am comforted that the Holy Spirit intercedes for me (Romans 8:26) and by how often He gives me the words to pray once I begin. I also enjoy taking a verse from Scripture and praying it for my husband (who is also named Paul), like Psalm 34:8, "Let Paul taste and see that the Lord is good; blessed is Paul when he takes refuge in You."

Sometimes I use prayer guides, like the one included later in this book. Spending time in prayer for my husband not only blesses him, but grows my relationship with him and with God. How can you pray for your husband today?

Tobi Henschel

Lord, I lift up to You my husband. Give him Your grace to face whatever comes today. Grow his love and passion for You that He can serve You well. Amen.

The Importance of Being Generous   *28*

You will be enriched in every way to be generous in every way, which through us will produce thanksgiving to God.

2 Corinthians 9:11

I want to be generous because God has given so lavishly to me through His people that I want to do the same. As the definition of *generous* states, I want to be ready "to give more than is strictly necessary or expected."

But, let's face it, it's so much easier to be stingy and selfish.

Instead of hoarding my time, money, and possessions, I want to learn to give freely to people who may need a listening ear, financial assistance, or a gift of encouragement. Being generous requires a different way of thinking. I must stop looking at myself — my needs and wants — and start thinking of others. I pray that God will open my eyes to see where He can use me in very simple ways.

Have extra garden produce? Don't let it rot, but give it away! Have some extra time? Make the rhubarb-strawberry jelly and give it away! Or freeze the extra corn and applesauce, and give it away!

Have you read a good book lately? Pass it on to someone you think will enjoy the book, too, without worrying if you get it back.

Want to go for a walk? Stop by and ask your friend if she'd like to walk with you. Take time to listen to her and enjoy her company.

Do some of your flowers and plants need thinning? Ask your friend if (and where) she'd like them — and plant them for her!

Get out of your pew and sit beside the one who is going through some struggles. Listen as she unloads. Pray for her.

Drop a little extra into the offering plate, and pray for God to use it abundantly.

God is changing my perspective and showing me how to be a blessing to others. Often, a thought will pop into my head to ask someone to lunch, or to make a call, or to send a card. I know it is from the Lord because that's not normally how I think. And what a blessing He gives when you know you have helped someone along the way! I'm praying that as you read this today, you will think of ways you can bless others.

And that God will bless you.

Lynnette Goebel

Heavenly Father, open our eyes, our hearts, and our hands today. Help us to give generously in Your Name. Amen.

"Do not be afraid of them, for I am with you to deliver you, declares the LORD." Then the LORD put out his hand and touched my mouth. And the LORD said to me, "Behold, I have put my words in your mouth."

Jeremiah 1:8-9

I distinctly remember the day God gave me a message for my ministry as a wife to my preacher-husband. I was kneeling over the homemade quilt which covered our bed, the quilt that my aunt and cousin lovingly sewed for our wedding gift a short year earlier. As I knelt and prayed in that tiny seminary campus apartment, God spoke clearly of my purpose in our future ministry as the preacher's wife: "Make him shine."

When we consider the lives of the prophets in Scripture, from Moses to Elijah, and Jeremiah, and even Christ Himself, we might have visions of a glorious pastoral ministry with people flocking to hear our great preacher-husbands.

The truth is that the majority of the messages that the prophets preached were ones of judgment and wrath, not of flowery words leaving the hearers feeling good about themselves. These men were persecuted in every way. Our husbands can experience the same thing, so they need us to support them and hold them up in this sacred and often difficult calling.

So…how can we as wives of prophets make their pulpit ministries shine? We need to know our God and His Word.

We need to love and know our God by cultivating intimacy with Him and knowing His Word. We have to know and study the Word of God ourselves if we are going to be sounding boards that our husbands can use to test their ideas throughout their study during the week.

I find joy when I'm listening to my husband's messages because, first of all, God uses his gifts to shepherd me, but it is also encouraging when something he shares from the pulpit reflects some of the thoughts that I've shared with him in his preparations. That assures me that our discussions about the Scripture have enabled him to better communicate the message to our people.

I may not be the one speaking up front each week, but I know that by knowing my God and knowing His Word, I have been able to love my preacher-husband and make his preaching ministry shine.

Wendy McCready

God, make me a helper to my preacher-husband and empower me to serve You in the ministry of the Word. Keep me faithfully seeking to know You and Your Word so that I can encourage him and bless You. Amen.

Therefore take up the whole armor of God, that you may be able to withstand in the evil day, and having done all, to stand firm.
Ephesians 6:13

"*D*oes this dress make me look fat?" Much has been made about the fact that there is no right answer for a husband whose wife asks this question. I have felt that way, too, over the years when my husband would ask me after a sermon, "How did I do?" I still remember one Sunday afternoon early on in our ministry lives when I said the "wrong" thing. It left him feeling discouraged and me feeling like an awful wife.

Even after all these years, I still struggle sometimes to know how I can really help my husband with his sermons. He is so vulnerable after he finishes preaching, yet he always wants to improve and so asks for my input.

To love our preacher-husbands, we have to know our own husband's specific needs and ask him what will help him most after a sermon.

We also need to know our husband's calling. The reality is that our husbands stand up each week, pouring out their hearts and souls, making themselves vulnerable in a way that is going to open them up to all kinds of responses.

The parable of the soil is very clear that people will respond to the Word in different ways, and three out of the four are negative! The same people who are praising your husband's sermon one week may be openly (or secretly) criticizing his preaching the next week.

As the wife of the preacher, you need to be cognizant of the spiritual battle your husband fights. Have listening ears and speak the truth lovingly without criticizing him when he finishes preaching each week. You can be a filter for him so that he can discern which criticism he receives is worth listening to and which needs to be tossed out.

If you do that, you will be loving your preacher-husband well after the sermon.

Wendy McCready

Heavenly Father, You know the battle we face every day as we serve Your church. Help me to put on the full armor to stand against the Enemy and to stand firm in prayer for my husband as he preaches Your Word with boldness and faith. Amen.

Joy

For His anger is but for a moment, and His favor is for a lifetime. Weeping may tarry for the night, but joy comes with the morning.

Psalm 30:5

*J*oy is a by-product of the hard times in life. I once heard of a couple who lost their house to fire. They lost almost everything, but they found a mug that had been made for them. How did it survive when other things burned up? They remembered their friend saying he had put it in a kiln and fired it. It survived because it had already been through a fire; it had passed through the heat and therefore was able to take more fire.

Every fire of refinement God brings into our lives enables us to withstand the further fires! God allows us, even plans for us, to go through the heat, not to destroy us or to hurt us, but to make us stronger.

And then comes the joy, more deeply experienced because of the fire that refined us.

David says in Psalm 16:11, "You make known to me the path of life; in your presence there is fullness of joy." Fullness of joy, the cry of my heart, is found in His presence. So, when I pursue Him and stay in His presence, there is joy!

As we explore joy over the next thirty days, may this cry of David's become ours as well.

Lois Seadore

Idolatry: The Thief of Joy   *31*

Cast me not away from your presence, and take not your Holy Spirit from me. Restore to me the joy of your salvation, and uphold me with a willing spirit.

Psalm 51:11-12

I struggle with idolatry, the ultimate thief of joy. It is a daily reality that pulls my heart away from the worship of my Lord to the worship of those things which entice me. It is an ever-looming, always painful battle that, when won, brings clarity and worship for my Lord. Yet when the battle is lost, it provides momentary, false control only to be followed by anguish.

These idols produced of my own heart steal away the joy of the Lord with a stealth unmatched by anything in this world. It is not stone statues, offerings to be burned, or strange ideas of the universe that steal my heart away from Him. Instead, it is the gifts, blessings, and moments He has given that I hold onto far too tightly. My own heart perverts the focus of my worship and draws me away from the Giver.

He gives my children—I teach them good behavior for my own pride instead of His glory, crippling their influence and growth. He gives my home—I fuss and fume that the improvements will never be good enough, missing opportunities to show hospitality. He gives my ministry—I hold it too dearly, accept praise too readily, and forget His hand too easily, causing fruitless effort.

And so, idolatry steals my joy, draws me in, and entraps my heart and flesh. "For all that is in the world—the desires of the flesh and the desires of the eyes and pride of life—is not from the Father but is from the world" (1 John 2:16).

Yet, in His gentle, ever-loving, never-failing way, He whispers through His Word, "Humble yourself, confess your sins, and abide in My love" (1 Peter 5:6; 1 John 1:8; 4:16).

Then as the Holy Spirit once again rescues my thoughts, pulls back my heart from the depths, and entreats me to pray, "Restore to me the joy of your salvation" (Psalm 51:12a), His Word proves ever true.

Sarah Chadbourn

Lord, I come to you humbled from the entrapments of my heart idols, yet confident in Your forgiveness and love. Help me so strongly to abide in Your love that I may find only discomfort in idols and only comfort in Your presence. Amen.

Do nothing from rivalry or conceit, but in humility count others
more significant than yourselves....Have this mind among your-
selves, which is yours in Christ Jesus.

Philippians 2:3, 5

$\mathcal{R}$eluctance is one of my biggest joy stealers. Once I start focusing on myself, I can quickly lose the bigger picture of seeing sacrifices for my church family as participation in God's
kingdom work. Before vocational ministry, I was eager to par-
ticipate in the mundane parts of church life. Now I notice it is
easier to negatively focus on the label and responsibility of
"pastor."

On one occasion we agreed last-minute it would be good for
my pastor-husband to attend the evening missionary event —
on his night off! I was not excited about the idea. When the
time came for my husband to leave, I wanted to be happy, but
I was not. My reluctant heart started rearing its ugly head,
and my joy rushed out the door into the cold night right behind him.

"Why does he get to socialize and pray while I have to clean
up and put the kids to bed by myself?!"

My response to the situation was not satisfying, and it was
not God-honouring either. When he arrived home again, we
discussed the scenario surrounding my pity-party for one.
My joy-thieving attitude was identified as *reluctance.*

The root of my reluctant heart was discontentedness. I so often want something different from what I have. Do you find
that, too? We want to trade in our cards instead of joyfully

serving and using ministry challenges and trials to grow our perseverance and character.

Giving up husband and daddy to ministry needs, especially unexpected ones, can be a great sacrifice. Maybe you are like I am and it does not immediately occur to you that evening meetings or long phone calls from home are not your husband's first choice either! When we acknowledge our husband's challenge to serve joyfully, we can extend empathy. Instead of seeing our husband or ministry as the problem, we can fight side by side against our reluctant hearts, asking God for the help we so desperately need.

Resisting reluctance also acknowledges the advantages of ministry. It may be easier to announce the disadvantages of being married to the pastor, but we must not be blind to the joys. Identifying and thanking the Lord for the blessings and privileges of ministry — including the eternal ones — encourages our own hearts, impacts our attitudes and actions, and honours the Lord.

Nicole Martin

Lord Jesus, I need Your help to humbly choose the perspective of service, following Your example of sacrifice. Strengthen me with endurance and patience so I can minister and walk through life with contentment and joy! Amen.

For You, O LORD, have made me glad by what You have done, I will sing for joy at the works of Your hands.

Psalm 92:4 NASB

During our Vacation Bible School training, we talked about the importance of being attentive. The trainer asked us to watch a video of two jugglers and count the number of times they threw a red ball back and forth between them. I dutifully focused on the ball and counted up my total: seventeen times.

Then the trainer asked us how many of us had noticed the gorilla. I blinked at her. I had watched that video—there was no gorilla in the crowd. I was sure of it! But when she played the video again, I saw she was right. In the middle of the video, someone dressed in a gorilla costume wandered into the crowd behind the jugglers, waved at the camera, and exited the scene. I'd been so focused on the ball that I had missed the gorilla.

There's actually a term for this phenomenon: inattentional blindness. It has to do with how our brain works to filter stimuli. We can't focus on everything, so our brains help us filter out what's important. We can be so focused on one thing that we miss other details—even when those details are as obvious as an out-of-place gorilla.

I've found that I can have inattentional blindness in ministry, too. It happens when I get so caught up in making sure the Bible School decorations are perfect that I forget to rejoice over the three new families who came last night. Or when I'm so worried over the conflict and complainers that I miss the girl in the third row who senses a call to ministry.

It happens when I fret over my weaknesses, forgetting to rely on God's power. When I focus on the wrong things, I miss the right thing—seeing God at work around me.

I can overcome my inattentional blindness by intentionally focusing on what God is doing. What is God teaching me? Whose life is He transforming? What is God up to in my world, and how can I join Him? When I spot those things, it reminds me both to rejoice and to invite others to celebrate with me. God is at work in my world. That's cause for joy.

Leigh Powers

Lord, open my eyes to what You are doing around me. Focus my attention on where You are at work, and remind me to rejoice as I join You there. Amen.

Whatever you do, work heartily, as for the Lord and not for men, knowing that from the Lord you will receive the inheritance as your reward. You are serving the Lord Christ.

Colossians 3:23-24

*E*arly in ministry, we were given some advice from an uncle of mine who was also a pastor: "Don't let ministry cause you to neglect your family." He explained how he had regular family time pre-scheduled into his calendar so he could always tell someone, "I'm sorry, I have an appointment that evening," if necessary. Essentially, he was telling us the importance of saying *no* sometimes.

Have you ever felt as if you aren't allowed to say *no*? I'm a people pleaser and feel obligated to always say yes. As a pastor's wife, I worry that saying *no* will reflect badly on my husband. We are in ministry together, and it is a joy to serve; therefore, I should be ready to serve all the time, right? Or sometimes I think (like Elijah) that I have to say *yes* because there's no one else to do it.

However, I have learned that sometimes I need to say *no* to keep the joy of ministry — to not overcommit, burn out, or let my family suffer because there's nothing left for them. I have also learned that when God is leading me to say *no*, I need to trust that He has a plan and people to fulfill that plan, so it's not all up to me to fix everything.

So then is the answer to say *no* to all ministry opportunities? No! Every decision needs to be prayerfully considered. My husband and I also look at our family calendar and weigh out how much we are already committed to—ministry obligations for each of us, school events, or other things in our children's lives, and also time set aside purely for our family to be together.

Considering these questions and spending time praying helps me to know whether or not God is leading me to say *yes*. Yes or no, my joy in serving comes from knowing that I am serving the Lord, not men, and am accountable to Him (Colossians 3:23-24).

Are there areas in your life where God is leading you to say *no* or *yes*, and you need to listen?

Tobi Henschel

*Father, please give me wisdom to know what opportunities to say **yes** to, and when to say **no**. Help me to serve You well whether it is at church, at home, or in my community. Amen.*

Therefore be imitators of God, as beloved children. And walk in love, as Christ loved us and gave himself up for us, a fragrant offering and sacrifice to God.

Ephesians 5:1-2

One Christmas my daughter came home from school with a canning jar she'd decorated and a spider plant already growing in it. The plant grew so well that eventually the roots became so entangled. I couldn't get it out of the jar without damaging it, so I left it. Deep roots are like that: the longer they are, the more pain in the pulling up and replanting.

When I look back at my initial challenge to step out in God's call to be a pastor's wife, it hurt to say *yes* mostly because I have deep rural roots with a lot of extended family members close by, and it hurt to have those roots pulled up.

I keenly recall the evening I knelt by my dorm room bedside as a young woman with my favorite family photo resting in my open hands. I knew God was asking me to obey His call to go wherever He asked, even if it meant not going back "home" to minister or having the approval or understanding of my family.

I didn't fully understand the implications of what that sacrifice would require of me, but I knew my love for God had to supersede all other loves. That meant some tearing up and rooting up; some pain was going to come, but that path leads to blessing, no matter if you are a pastor's wife or not.

I have the blessings of peace deep in my soul, knowing I have allowed God to be first place. I have the opportunity to expand my love for the people whom God has created who are different from me, and I have learned the joy of participating in the sufferings of Christ. I can endure the sufferings, knowing the joy that is before me, like Christ did.

Who was more misunderstood? Who faced greater temptations? Who knew what it was like to leave the most perfect home and family that ever existed? And what has He done for me? How can I sacrifice any less?

Oh, and that plant in the jar? I never did get to transplant it. Do you know what happened? The roots rotted in the jar and became putrid and died. Sometimes we have to be transplanted to grow.

Wendy McCready

Lord, the last thing I want to do is to become complacent. Help me to trust You, even when growth requires sacrifice and pain. Make me useful to Your service wherever You plant me. Amen.

Therefore, if anyone is in Christ, the new creation has come: The old has gone, the new is here!

2 Corinthians 5:17 NIV

To know your identity means to know your true self. Outside of Christ, there are many things we can focus on to describe who we are: our job, marital status, number of children, personality type, social network, etc. But knowing who you are in Christ changes how you view every aspect of your life.

How we see ourselves is often revealed in how we introduce ourselves. We feel the need to explain to people that what we do and our accomplishments are significant. But the comparison game will always rob us of joy.

Elisabeth Elliot said, "The fact that I am a woman does not make me a different kind of Christian, but the fact that I am a Christian makes me a different kind of woman." My identity, found in my relationship with Christ, has been the anchor through every changing season no matter what is added to or subtracted from my current resume.

I am not defined by the things that I do but by who I am in Christ. He calls me His beloved, His child, His chosen one; I am enough, I am forgiven, I am free. The Biblical understanding of identity guards my heart and mind and makes even the most mundane task in my day something that can be used for His glory.

How do you see yourself? If you don't see yourself the way Christ sees you, viewed through the lens of His righteousness, the enemy sees you as vulnerable prey to deceive with all manner of lies. If you don't know the inheritance you have in Christ, the devil is stalking you like a lion waiting to devour you. The only way to discover your true identity is to let God tell you through His Word. The Bible tells us the absolute truth of who we are in Christ. Every aspect of our lives will have eternal purpose when viewed through the lens of our identity in Christ!

Chelsea Hall

Lord, help me to see myself the way You see me; give me an eternal perspective. Help me to guard my heart and mind so that even the most mundane tasks that I do throughout the day become something You use for Your glory! Amen.

For His anger is but for a moment, His favor is for a lifetime; Weeping may last for the night, But a shout of joy comes in the morning.
Psalm 30:5 NASB

Sometimes life just goes on day after day, always the same. As an introvert and perfectionist, normal days that go by without any disruption are considered a favorite for me. Don't throw extra work at me. Don't move up a due date. Don't add drama to my life.

Sometimes disaster strikes, and life just goes on day after day. Things are different, but it still goes on. I remember walking out of the hospital after my mother passed out of this life into her eternal life. I could not figure out why the birds were singing or why the sun was shining. It didn't seem right that things kept on day after day.

Sometimes, in the middle of those day-after-day moments, God sends a love note that results in shouts of joy.

- *Walking in from the car, looking up, and seeing the beautiful harvest moon*

- *Driving to work and noticing a majestic hawk soaring overhead*

- *Reaching into the mailbox and finding a special note from a friend*

- *Looking up from reading to notice a nuthatch at the feeder and a downy woodpecker in the tree*

- *Waking early in the morning to see a glorious sunrise*

- *Answering the phone to hear a little voice say, "Hi Gamma!"*

- *Reading Psalm 121 and feeling the security of God's arms*

- *Hearing the doctor say, "Everything looks good!"*

- *Finding that item for which you've searched for days*

- *Finding that item you had forgotten you had*

- *Listening to the voices of your church family praising God*

- *Hearing the voices of children praising God around a campfire*

- *Eating the perfect S'more*

- *Receiving words of affirmation that warm you to your toes*

How do you respond to the love notes that God sends your way? With a shout of joy? A prayer of thanksgiving? Or do you even notice them in the busyness of today?

Lynnette Goebel

Heavenly Father, today I ask that each busy pastor's wife will notice the sweet notes of love You send her way. Make her aware of Your presence. Give her the time to stop and be refreshed. May her heart be full of rejoicing as she lays her head on her pillow tonight because she has seen the gifts from Your hands and heart of love. Amen.

As each has received a gift, use it to serve one another, as good stewards of God's varied grace.

1 Peter 4:10

𝒫salm 100:1-2 says, "Make a joyful noise to the Lord, all the earth! Serve the Lord with gladness!" So why is it often a struggle for us to serve the Lord with gladness? Maybe it is because we approach service the wrong way. We look for what will make us happy or will please others, and we think that is how to serve joyfully. But there is a better way.

First, consider what your gifts are—both your talents and your spiritual gifts. Are you musical? Are you good with kids? Are you handy? You might have the spiritual gift of wisdom, faith, helping, administrating, prophecy, or teaching. Look at how God has gifted you uniquely, and see where you can use those gifts in your church. Using our gifts as God intended can bring us (and others) great joy!

But what happens when there isn't a perfect fit for your gifts in your church? Or maybe you (or others) wish you had certain gifts that you don't? For example, I am a pastor's wife who can't play the piano—tragic, I know! So, does that mean I can't serve effectively? Certainly not! Service isn't just about us and how we're gifted—if we treat it this way, we will quickly become disappointed by other people, by circumstances, and by ourselves.

At the end of 1 Corinthians 12, when Paul has been talking about spiritual gifts and the body of Christ working together, he says in verse 31, "And I will show you a still more excellent way." This leads into 1 Corinthians 13, "The Love Chapter."

I get chills just thinking about this—God has given us great gifts (both spiritual ones and talents), but in the end Paul says that the "still more excellent way" is *love*. Serving God and others in love is the way to find joy in serving.

Take a moment to read through 1 Corinthians 13 with this question in mind: How can I serve God joyfully?

Tobi Henschel

God, please show me where you want me to serve today. No matter what area it is, fill me with Your love that I may serve You with joy! Amen.

O God, you are my God; earnestly I seek you; my soul thirsts for you; my flesh faints for you, as in a dry and weary land where there is no water.

Psalm 63:1

"You're married to the pastor; what do you have to be depressed about?" Nobody has ever said this to me, but I can imagine it happening. "You've got a happy family, a nice home, a steady job, why are you complaining?" The voice in my head goes on and on and doesn't contain an ounce of grace or compassion.

I get depressed. No matter how hard I try, I sink inward, down deep inside myself. I stop feeling much of anything, and I watch life swirl on around me without fully engaging in it. I go through the motions, of course, but I feel personally disconnected from family, friends, and life itself. It is extremely isolating. I would prefer to feel something, anything really, but I don't. Nobody knows that on the inside I am isolated and untouched by all the turmoil of life that swirls around me.

When I get depressed, I can commiserate with David calling out to God in the Psalms. I know God is listening, hearing my cries, seeing my despair, but I am still lost and calling on Him to show me the way out.

The more I think about the impacts of my depression, the more guilt I feel. It is a vicious cycle. Depression causes guilt, and guilt causes me to feel more depressed. I try so hard to dig myself out because I like to be in charge.

I don't want to admit that I can't do one solitary thing to help myself, but it is here, when I reach my lowest point, that I realize the one thing, the best thing, I can do is to hand everything over to God.

It is so easy for me to forget that it is only when I let go and wait on the Lord that I am renewed. I can never do it myself. Isaiah 40:31 says, "But they who wait for the LORD shall renew their strength; they shall mount up with wings like eagles; they shall run and not be weary; they shall walk and not faint." I have learned how important it is to wait. God in His goodness will lift me out of my despair, but I must wait on Him rather than relying on my own strength.

Marcy Ardis

Dear Lord, help me to hand my burdens over to You. You, and only You, know how lost I feel right now. Help me to remember to rely on Your strength rather than dwelling on my own imperfections. Amen.

I Am Not Alone: 40
Finding Balance in the Depths of Depression

I will sing to the Lord as long as I live; I will sing praise to my God while I have being.

Psalm 104:33

If I'm going to function well every day, I need to spend quiet, uninterrupted time with God. The problem is, I just don't have much silence in my day. I know I'm not the only person facing this dilemma.

The only time I can find silence is early in the morning. I sit in silence in my favourite room, in my favourite spot, with my cat on my lap. The most important thing, though, is that I sit in the presence of God.

As part of my morning routine, I read several devotionals and the Bible. I also pray, sometimes in my head, sometimes out loud, and sometimes through writing in my journal. I sit quietly and listen for what God may want to say to me. In the silence of the morning, I often do hear His voice, whether through a particularly poignant Bible passage, a thought of encouragement, or by some bit of clarity written in the pages of my journal.

Psalm 104 describes God in all His splendour. The all-powerful God of this universe is my Father. He loves me and He loves you. When I am lost in the midst of the despair of my depression, I know that He has not, and will not, abandon me. Even in the midst of my depression, I know the joy of being at peace with God through the process of laying my burdens at His feet.

Spending daily time with God doesn't take away my depression, but it helps me manage it. It helps me to let go and place my depression, my worries, and my isolation in God's hands. He is Lord, and He is in control. He will hold me in the palm of His hand throughout my distress.

Marcy Ardis

Lord, I know that I can do nothing without You. You are my strength when I am weak, and You hold me up when I am sure that I cannot stand on my own. Grant me Your peace today. Let the people I encounter see You reflected in all of my actions. Amen.

Therefore I will boast all the more gladly of my weaknesses, so that the power of Christ may rest upon me.

2 Corinthians 12:9b

*M*y role as a pastor's wife is the realization of a childhood dream. As a little girl, I would pretend to be in ministry as I played "church." I prayed for my husband long before I knew him, and in faith I asked God to prepare me to be a pastor's wife one day. And God did just that. He answered my prayer and gave me the desires of my heart. And it has been a beautiful thing.

What I did not expect was the debilitating panic attacks that became a part of my life at the age of 19 at almost the same time that God brought my husband, Ben, to me. The first panic attack came out of the blue, and that panic attack set off two decades of relentless panic.

Because of these attacks I understand the desperation of feeling helpless and hopeless. I know what it's like to plead with God and wonder if He hears me. I have felt inefficient and ineffective. I've pondered how lacking I am as a pastor's wife. I know the feelings of loss and dreams dashed. I have been accused by the enemy and tempted to believe that I could never serve Christ, as flawed as I am.

If you find yourself in my same position, and you feel as if your ministry is overtaken by a deficit that is bigger than you can fathom or handle, I want you to know that our God is bigger! He's stronger and He's mightier than the panic attacks. He's able. He will sustain you, and He will carry you.

But He said to me, "My grace is sufficient for you, for my power is made perfect in weakness" (II Corinthians 12:9).

Does panic affect my ministry? Absolutely. But has it taken away my ability to minister to others joyfully? Absolutely not.

God can give you joy through the trial of panic and anxiety in your life and ministry. It really is possible because we serve the God of the impossible!

Amber Fox

Lord of Peace, You have called me, weaknesses and all, to be a vessel of Your grace. Use me for Your glory, and even in the pain and struggle, give me joy in You. Amen.

He will tend his flock like a shepherd; he will gather the lambs in his arms; he will carry them in his bosom, and gently lead those that are with young.

Isaiah 40:11

We all reach a point where we need to rest. Maybe it is after a long day of hard work or maybe after a particularly difficult encounter with a friend or family member. Often our fatigue is simply due to the day-to-day events that can lead to stress and burnout if we don't take some time to step back and refresh ourselves in quietness in the presence of God.

Isaiah 40:31 reminds us to "wait for the Lord" to renew our strength. This verse reminds me of the perfect peace that can be found in the centre of God's will. It is an acknowledgement of my weakness and how it is made perfect in His strength.

I love the specificity of this verse. If we wait for the Lord, we will be rewarded. When we seek God's will and follow His direction, we are given untold freedom to soar as eagles.

We are not told what waiting for the Lord looks like. It certainly encompasses listening for God's direction in our lives and trusting that His way is best. When we trust God's plan for our lives and follow the path that He has chosen for us, we find peace, and, when we are at peace, we can rest, knowing that God is in control.

Throughout Isaiah 40 we read of God's awe-inspiring majesty and strength, but we also read of His tender care for His people. Isaiah 40:11 says, "He will tend his flock like a shepherd; he will gather the lambs in his arms; he will carry them in his bosom, and gently lead those that are with young."

Can you picture anything more tender than this? Our God, the same God who created the universe and everything in it, tenderly cradles His most vulnerable and precious children in His bosom, close to His heart. There are many days when this is exactly where I yearn to be.

Don't we all feel vulnerable and in need of protection some-times? Don't we all yearn to be held safely sometimes? This is exactly what God does for us, and, when He feels we are ready, we can soar like eagles in the freedom of His perfect plan.

Marcy Ardis

Dear Lord, I am tired and I can't keep going on my own strength. Renew my strength as I rest in the safety of Your protection. Thank You for the peace of knowing that You have a perfect plan set in place for my life. Amen.

And an angel of the Lord appeared to them, and the glory of the Lord shone around them, and they were filled with fear. And the angel said to them, "Fear not, for behold, I bring you good news of great joy that will be for all the people. For unto you is born this day in the city of David a Savior, who is Christ the Lord.

Luke 2:9-11

When it's the time of year for Christmas movies, my absolute favorite is *A Charlie Brown Christmas*. I still get chills during the speech that Linus gives when Charlie Brown asks if anyone knows what the true meaning of Christmas is. Linus responds by quoting from Luke 2 and telling Charlie Brown, "That's what Christmas is all about."

I've always loved reading Luke 2, whether during the Advent season or any time of the year, and meditating on the amazing happenings of that wondrous night. As I read the passage, two emotions stand out—great fear and great joy.

When the angels appear in the sky, the shepherds are filled with great fear. It seems obvious at first why they would be afraid—they are witnessing a supernatural, mind-blowing event. Heaven has been ripped open, and they're glimpsing something beyond their wildest imaginations.

But even more than that, they are being confronted with holiness, with a reminder of their sin and how far short of God's standard they fall. They're looking heavenly beings in the eye and seeing firsthand that they don't meet the standard. They should be afraid!

Then the angel turns the tables and tells them, "Fear not, for behold, I bring you good news of great joy" (v. 10). In their moment of **greatest fear**, they are being given the **greatest joy**. What is that joy? Good news that will be for all the people — a Savior has been born! In that moment when the shepherds are face to face with their inadequacy, the angel gives them the good news that they don't have to be adequate because the Savior has been born, the One who will meet the standard for us.

Don't be afraid. Soak in that joyful truth: you don't have to be good enough — in fact, you can't be good enough — because the Savior has been born, and He will meet God's perfect standard on our behalf.

Have you been feeling inadequate for our Lord? What do you need to turn over today to receive that joy?

Tobi Henschel

Jesus, thank You for meeting the standard for me. I confess to You my inadequacy and praise You for Your righteousness given on my behalf! Amen.

For everything there is a season, and a time for every matter under heaven...a time to weep, and a time to laugh; a time to mourn, and a time to dance.

Ecclesiastes 3:1, 4

Tears come easily to me. Happy or sad, I cry.

When I watched movies as a child, my dad and brother teased me about the tears. As a result, I tried to steel myself against crying. But then I never fully threw myself into the plot. I held myself aloof from the characters. I hardened my heart.

Many people apologize when tears fall as they share their struggles and pains. God created us to cry, and we should not apologize for our tears. I want people to feel comfortable talking with me, sharing their joys and sorrows with me. How can I be an encouragement if they cannot share from the depth of their beings?

Tears come as a result of stress, suffering, mourning, pain, anger, happiness, fear, laughter, frustration, or remorse. I've gone through times where it seemed I cried all the tears out of me and would never cry again. Other times I ached for the tears to come to relieve the stress and pressure building inside of me.

I understand the admonition in Scripture to "weep with those who weep." I do not want to hold back but throw myself into the lives of the people God puts in my path. If they rejoice, I must rejoice. If they weep, I weep.

Looking through the Bible, we see that Abraham (Genesis 23:2), Jacob (Genesis 29:11), Joseph (Genesis 43:30), and David

(1 Samuel 20:41) wept at great sorrow in their lives. The prophets wept over the state of Israel, and Jesus wept at the death of Lazarus (John 11:35).

Oh, that God will give us hearts that are willing to share in the pain of others, to weep for the lost, and to intercede for the burdened! May we be like Job where *"my intercessor is my friend as my eyes pour out tears to God"* (Job 16:20 NIV). Let them not only be tears for ourselves, but for others.

Lynnette Goebel

Heavenly Father, give us compassionate hearts. If one of our pastors' wives is hurting, please send a comforter her way to share her burden, to weep with her, and to pray with her. Thank You for the gift of tears. Amen.

The Lasting Legacy of Aquila and Priscilla: 45
Part One

And he [Paul] found a Jew named Aquila, a native of Pontus, recently come from Italy with his wife Priscilla, because Claudius had commanded all the Jews to leave Rome. ...And because he was of the same trade he stayed with them and worked.

Acts 18:2-3a

$\mathcal{T}$hree great examples of pastoral couples who together have left lasting legacies are Billy and Ruth Graham, Tony and Lois Evans, and Aquila and Priscilla of the New Testament. "Two are better than one" was certainly true of Aquila and Priscilla, who are always mentioned together in the Word of God. They were close friends with the Apostle Paul, sharing both the trade of tentmaking and the joy of disciple-making.

Through the eighteen years that pass in the life of this couple from the time Paul meets them in AD 49 until he mentions them shortly before his martyrdom in AD 67, we see a lasting ministry legacy through six life-actions we will explore in the next few days.

At least four times in Scripture they **moved** from one place to another. Perhaps the most challenging for Priscilla is recorded in Acts 18:2a, "And he found a Jew named Aquila, a native of Pontus, recently come from Italy with his wife Priscilla." They left her hometown and moved 992.97 km/536.16 nautical miles to Corinth, Greece.

I've set up home five times since marrying my farmer-called-to-be-a-pastor husband in 2001. Have you ever asked your pastor's wife how many times she's said goodbye to people, places, and ministries? I drag my feet every time; every time God gives joy in the new normal.

They **worked** together as tentmakers, building, sweating, sewing, repairing—true life partners! Shortly after their big move from Italy to Greece, Paul *"went to see them, and because he was of the same trade he stayed with them and worked, for they were tentmakers by trade"* (Acts 18:2b-3). These three made a great tent-building, joy-filled, Gospel-sharing team.

Denna Busenitz

Lord God, fill me with joy through whatever moves You ask of my husband and me. Let me say goodbye well and embrace what You have for me at each place of service. Thank You for the privilege of being my husband's life-partner in the work You call us to. Amen.

The Lasting Legacy of Aquila and Priscilla: 46
Part Two

*Aquila and Prisca, together with the church in their house, send you
hearty greetings in the Lord.*

1 Corinthians 16:19b

$\mathcal{N}$ot only did Aquila and Priscilla move and work together,
they also **traveled** together. Whole marketing careers are focused on getting people to travel for leisure. It was starkly different for Aquila and Priscilla. They often traveled together,
many times with Paul, not for fun (though I imagine they
laughed a lot!), but always with the same two-pronged goal
of evangelism and discipleship.

Having been in rural and small-town church-planting ministry for almost two decades, I can say that my husband and I
have put a lot of miles on four-wheel drive vehicles and he on
a horse. Aquila and Priscilla traveled by boat for greater dis-
tances, however, leaving behind familiar faces each time to
make Christ known in the next town and the next.

Their travels bore much spiritual fruit. This Jewish couple's
impact sailed across cultural lines: "Not only I [Paul] give
thanks but all the churches of the Gentiles give thanks as
well" (Romans 16:4b).

When they stopped traveling, they **hosted** together. It's encouraging to know Priscilla found time to host amidst her
daily tent-making work. No doubt she kept things simple yet
meaningful.

Charles Keeler wrote *The Simple Home* in 1906 saying, "The
ideal home is one in which the family may be most completely

sheltered to develop in love, graciousness, and individuality, and which is at the same time most accessible to friends, toward whom hospitality is as unconscious and spontaneous as it is abundant."

My husband loves to have people in our home and gives me the extra nudge I often need. We host best together. Aquila and Priscilla hosted Paul (Acts 18:3), church fellowships (Romans 16:3-5a; 1 Corinthians 16:19), and people like Apollos who benefited from their counsel (Acts 18:26).

Paul's use of the phrase *hearty greetings* in 1 Corinthians 16:19b describes the vibrant personality of the house-church that met at Aquila and Priscilla's. Similar words for *hearty* in the Scriptures are *loud*, *great*, and *many*. Corporate worship in their home was the impetus for this couple's lasting legacy. Priscilla and Aquila's home overflowed with the joy of the Lord.

Denna Busenitz

Lord God, may the joy of the Lord abound in our home today and always. Amen.

He [Apollos] began to speak boldly in the synagogue, but when Priscilla and Aquila heard him, they took him and explained to him the way of God more accurately.

Acts 18:26

*W*e have looked at how Priscilla and Aquila moved, worked, traveled, and hosted together. They also **counseled and discipled** together. This ministry couple had moved from Italy to Corinth and then to Ephesus when they met a Jew named Apollos. A native of Alexandria, Apollos had come to Ephesus "an eloquent man, competent in the Scriptures, ... instructed in the way of the Lord, ... fervent in spirit, he spoke and taught accurately the things concerning Jesus". Apollos was lacking one thing: "he knew only the baptism of John" (Acts 18:24-25).

Aquila and Priscilla took him (very likely into their home) and graciously explained the way of God more accurately. The next thing we know, Apollos is crossing the Aegean Sea to Achaia and the capital city, Corinth (Acts 19:1), with a letter commending his ministry to these people.

Apollos went on to become a powerful public debater and dynamic preacher, showing that Jesus was the Christ. This world needs more preachers like Apollos, but it also needs more ministry couples like Aquila and Priscilla who abide in God's Word and provide wise counsel to the next generation. Dear pastor's wife, be ready. God just might send the next Apollos to you and your husband.

They **risked their lives serving together**. Paul asks the Romans to "greet Priscilla and Aquila, my fellow workers in

Christ Jesus, who risked their necks for my life" (Romans 16:3-4a). He knew their risk for his sake would be of benefit to the many spiritual children that followed as he continued to boldly share the Gospel until his martyrdom in AD 67.

I picture Aquila and Priscilla having similar boldness as Paul's friends who lowered him in a basket through an opening in the city wall by night to escape certain death (Acts 9:23-25). Who could use unwavering courage today in the battle to share Christ?

Denna Busenitz

Lord God, unite my husband and me for the purposes of passing on godly counsel to others and risking everything to ensure the Gospel spreads in our area. Give us like-minded friends with whom we can serve You. Amen.

Do not be anxious about anything, but in everything by prayer and supplication with thanksgiving let your requests be made known to God. And the peace of God, which surpasses all understanding, will guard your hearts and your minds in Christ Jesus.

Philippians 4:6-7

My daughter suffers from anxiety, and fear has impacted her life for as long she can remember. Her anxiety can be all-consuming, and it means that, at the age when so many other children are starting to do things on their own, my daughter can't walk upstairs in our home without someone accompanying her. It means that she often calls out to see where we are located in our home so that she knows we are near. She fears being apart from us because, if we leave the house, something may happen to us and we will never come back to her. She misses out on so many things.

I cannot express how difficult it is to watch her struggle. Simple things like shaking hands and clapping bother her. She recognizes that her behaviour is different, and she does not want to be pointed out for her differences, but she has great difficulty controlling it.

First Peter 5:7 encourages us to cast all of our anxieties on Him, because He cares for us. Mornings are hard in our home, but, even in the chaos of anxiety, we want to encourage our daughter to turn to prayer, to place her worries and burdens in the hands of God.

When our daughter was younger, we prayed for her. Now that she is older, we pray together, and when her fear is overwhelming, she has started to ask us to lift her up in prayer.

I am so thankful that she recognizes that she can hand her worries and fears over to the God of all creation with the expectation and knowledge that He cares for her.

God commands us not to be anxious, but I won't lie. I worry about my daughter, and I don't have any answers. I only have hope. I place my hope in the Lord, and I know that as my daughter grows in her relationship with God, she will learn to rely on Him and experience peace even in the midst of her fears.

Marcy Ardis

Dear Lord, help me to be a good example of a godly woman for my children. Help me to be faithful in spending time in prayer and reading the Bible, not only for my own needs, but so that my children can see how important it is to rely on You rather than on their own strength. Amen.

Put on then, as God's chosen ones, holy and beloved, compassionate hearts, kindness, humility, meekness, and patience, bearing with one another and, if one has a complaint against another, forgiving each other; as the Lord has forgiven you, so you also must forgive. And above all these put on love, which binds everything together in perfect harmony.

Colossians 3:12-14

One Sunday morning I caught my daughter running in the sanctuary, and I said something along the lines of, "Your dad's the pastor. I don't want you running around like that. You need to show the other kids the right way to behave."

I suspect what she actually heard was, "You can't run and play and have fun like the rest of the kids because your daddy is the pastor. You need to be better than the rest of the kids." What an effective way for me to make attending church an unpleasant and unhappy experience for my daughter.

My daughter was seven at the time. Why, at the age of seven, did she need to be a role model for kids who are twice her age? The fact that her dad is the pastor should not preclude her from having fun just like the rest of the kids. Granted, I still don't want her running around in the sanctuary after church, but there are much better ways of explaining that to her.

As I started to contemplate what I had said, I realized the ungodliness that was inherent in the words I spoke to my daughter. I was not concerned about modeling grace and love to her, but rather my only concern was how her behaviour was reflecting on her dad and me.

What would people think about our parenting skills? Was the kid who just ran screeching past me with messy hair and her socks falling down really the pastor's kid?

I want my daughter to exhibit the traits that Paul has listed in Colossians. These are God-given expectations which will allow both my daughter and me to not only live, but thrive, as we walk together on the path God has chosen for our lives.

Marcy Ardis

Dear Lord, help me to be a model of Your grace and love in all my dealings with my children. Some days this is really hard to do, and I need your help to achieve it. May my children see You in all of my actions and in every word that comes out of my mouth. Amen.

And we know that for those who love God all things work together for good, for those who are called according to his purpose. For those whom he foreknew he also predestined to be conformed to the image of his Son, in order that he might be the firstborn among many brothers.

Romans 8:28-29

*M*aybe you or your kids have seen the movie *Inside Out*. It's the story of a girl named Riley and all of the feelings that live inside her mind and memories. Each feeling has a name and character, and the movie toggles between Riley's real life and the story that is running through her mind while life is playing out for her.

The red character is Anger. Joy, who tells the story, introduces him like this: "That's Anger. He cares very deeply about things being fair." And when they aren't fair? Well...he explodes — literally. A blowtorch-looking burst of fire shoots out of his head, and the screen flips back to Riley expressing her anger.

Many times, I have seen that blowtorch of anger shooting out of my PKs as they react to something that relates to our ministry life and role. Sadly, Anger and often Disgust, Sadness, and Fear visit them much more often than Joy does. Just like in the movie, I feel as if we are in the battle to keep Joy in the forefront.

But...as I raise my daughters, I've been challenged to think about life a bit like the conclusion of this movie.

In the end, the emotion characters and Riley learn that you can't have one emotion without the other – that they all work together to make up Riley's life experiences, which define and shape her in a way that wouldn't have as much meaning if everything were just Joy all the time.

We've tried to teach our daughters, even in the midst of tough moments when we feel our joy is being stolen, to remember Who is in charge, to have a forgiving heart, to know they are not alone, and to be thankful for the special blessings we have as a ministry family.

I guess it's a little like the *Inside Out* characters. At the end Joy concludes, "We've been through a lot," and "I think it's all beautiful." May our children say the same thing one day about growing up as the pastor's kids.

Wendy McCready

Lord, it is a privilege to serve Your church. Help my children to see our service as a blessing and not a burden. Help me to set an example of thankfulness, forgiveness, and love. Amen.

Greater love has no one than this, that someone lay down his life for his friends. You are my friends if you do what I command you. No longer do I call you servants, for the servant does not know what his master is doing; but I have called you friends, for all that I have heard from my Father I have made known to you.

John 15:13-15

I've been reading the biography of Lucy Maud Montgomery, author of the *Anne of Green Gables* series. If you haven't read the series, Anne is an orphan with a great imagination. One of the sorrows in her life was that she did not have a good friend, a kindred spirit. At one time in her life, she made friends with Katie, the girl who was a reflection in the glass door of the bookcase. Desperate for a friend, Anne imagined Katie and a whole world in which she lived.

The Lord has given me a few kindred spirits during my life. These are friends whom you know immediately upon meeting that they understand you. You feel an instant connection — as if you already know them. These friends are rare.

Much more common are the everyday friends who don't require deep intimacy but are always there when you need them. And you are there for them. Friendship grows over time as you attend school, church, or book club together. Circumstances put you in contact with each other, and looking back, you can see how your friendship grew. She's not someone you initially connected with, but after some time, you find that you have a good, cozy relationship.

Friendships seem to wax and wane. When we move miles away or families leave the church, we often feel as if our friendships are over.

However, they don't have to be. Don't give up! There are so many ways to stay friends these days.

But we must be intentional, keeping in touch through FaceTime, Zoom, sending an email, messaging on Facebook, sending small gifts or notes, praying for them. Break away from the old ideas of what friendship looks like, and let God open your eyes to new ways to be a friend. Be intentional!

Lynnette Goebel

Heavenly Father, sometimes ministry can be very lonesome for pastors' wives. I pray today that You will bring the right friends into their lives at the right time. Bring friends who love them, care for them, and encourage them. I ask that each pastor's wife would be intentional in growing her friendships into strong, cozy friendships.

And help them to remember that even when they feel alone, You are there, that You never leave them or forsake them. Amen.

Nehemiah said, "Go and enjoy choice food and sweet drinks, and send some to those who have nothing prepared. This day is holy to our Lord. Do not grieve, for the joy of the LORD is your strength."
Nehemiah 8:10 NIV

*T*he focus of Nehemiah 8:10b is normally on the Lord's strength keeping us happy. After all, we have a command in this partial verse to not be grieved but to be joyful.

If we dig into this verse, however, we find more than just reliance upon God to make everything just and right in our world. Notice it doesn't say *our* joy; it is the joy *of the Lord* that gives the Israelites strength.

The Israelites here are in the middle of repenting for their sins. Nehemiah, Ezra, and the Levite priests are absolving and instructing the Israelites of their guilt and shame. They were shown the law, they repented of their sins, and they went on to rejoice because they had understood the Word of the Lord.

God's joy is in the Israelites turning away from their sin. Their strength is rooted in God's grace instead of judgment being extended to this generation. God's Word was clear, it was explained, it was understood. God's Word was taken to heart, and lives were changed.

So how do we apply this to our lives, covered under the grace of Jesus?

God's joy comes from our repentant and contrite hearts when we turn away from sin. In giving all our cares, our struggles, and our pain to Jesus, we show our reliance on His joy for our strength. Our strength can be found in His grace, not in completing goals or in anything we do.

Cara Kipp

Dear Lord, give us joy that can only be found through serving and being obedient to You. Help us to reconcile the feelings of rebellion that encroach on our hearts and minds. We want to serve those around us with Your love and joy and mercy. Amen.

The joy of the LORD is your strength.

Nehemiah 8:10b

$\mathcal{M}$y fifth-grade English teacher had us write in our journals every day. In one entry I made a terrible attempt at writing a poem about cats. Every line ended with the word *is* or *are* or *were*. I can still see Mr. Winkler's bold, dark handwriting crossing out each of those "weak verbs," as he called them.

When it comes to the above verse, though, I beg to differ with my English teacher. The strongest word in this verse is the word *is*. It is the word that affirms the promise.

Nehemiah and Ezra are the speakers of these often-quoted words. They spoke the words at a time when the no-longer-exiled people of Israel had returned to Jerusalem, humbled and ready to rebuild. Ezra had just read the law of God to all those who could hear and understand, and they had listened attentively from early morning until midday!

When they heard the words of God, they responded by listening, standing up, lifting their hands and saying "Amen! Amen," bowing low, worshipping, and weeping (Nehemiah 8:6).

They had been living as captives in a foreign land for 70 years where they were influenced by a pagan culture and not exposed often to the Word of God. When they heard it read like this, they wept and mourned for how they had strayed. Surely, they must have wondered if God would still abandon them. Despite His covenant promises, would He forgive?

Nehemiah and Ezra called into the midst of this mourning with words of confidence that this day was holy to the LORD; they didn't need to mourn and weep, but they should be feasting and rejoicing. Why? Because "the joy of the LORD is your strength" (Nehemiah 8:9-10). They knew that God heard their repentant hearts and that He was ready to receive them with joy for their renewed worship of Him.

Friend, no matter your circumstances or how you've sinned, you can cling by faith to the promise of the great Self-Existent One. The Great I Am *is* your strength. He *is* your helper (Hebrews 13:6). He *is* your light and your salvation (Psalm 27:1). He *is* your rock; He *is* your fortress; He *is* your salvation (Psalm 62:2).

The joy of the Lord *is* your strength. Surely there is nothing weak about that.

Wendy McCready

Lord, all Your promises are sure. Forgive me for doubting You, and help me to rest in Your promises as I go about my day today. Amen.

The joy of the LORD is your strength.

Nehemiah 8:10b

A few years ago, in southwestern Ontario, we had one of the coldest winters recorded in 50 years. Preceding this deep and quick freeze was a spike in temperature that yielded such a deluge of rain and freezing rain that the ice it produced took down power lines all across our area and beyond, leaving many without power for weeks.

I will never forget lying in my bed in the dark with my daughters snuggled close to ward off the fear of the deep dark and cold, and the house devoid of any hum of fans or fridge running. It was eerie enough, and then...*crack*! A sound like a gunshot penetrated the quiet.

The deep cold had caused the ground to freeze so deeply that it was splitting deep beneath us. The local news reported the next day that so many people were concerned about these noises that they were calling the police!

The noises were called "frost-quakes." Quaking is what they made us do, and the whole experience made me grateful in so many ways for our home which provided us a place of safety and shelter from something over which we had no control.

So many different circumstances in our lives threaten to steal our joy or our security and sap us of strength. Some days we can only do the next thing as we stumble under the weight of fear, grief, pain, or suffering.

Not only can we count on joy in Him, but it will give us strength. The Hebrew word used here for *strength* signifies "a place or means of safety, protection." When we choose joy in our difficult circumstances, we have a place of safety, a refuge and defense from any harm.

We are kept by the Lord Himself, and He is all the strength we need to maintain our joy and gladness, even when the ground is literally quaking beneath us.

Wendy McCready

Almighty God, You are All-Powerful. I will rest in Your strength. I will choose joy. Amen.

If it had not been the LORD who was on our side — let Israel now say — if it had not been the LORD who was on our side when people rose up against us, then they would have swallowed us up alive. Our help is in the name of the LORD, who made heaven and earth.
                                                                Psalm 124:1-3a, 8

*T*wo of my kids were sick with a horrific virus that lasted for six weeks — a mother's worst nightmare. It was one of the lowest points in all my years of parenting.

I felt desperate to help them, and yet I couldn't. In my desperation, I cried out to God hourly as I watched my babies suffer with the most pain that I've ever seen anyone experience. I have a strong faith, and I know God hears our cries and sees our pain. Yet, in my deepest hour of need, He seemed silent. No answers came (at least from my human vantage point), and there was no relief from the pain.

Didn't God care? Why wouldn't He answer me? My deep-seeded faith, that I've carried with me since I was a small child, was challenged to the core. I've served Him faithfully, proclaimed His name, and dedicated my life to full-time ministry. Yet, God seemed silent.

Seemed. It's the operative word. I couldn't see or hear what God was doing, yet in His sovereign grace He gently and lovingly led me to Psalm 124 — a psalm of one who knows that God is our salvation and without Him, we are hopeless.

If God would not have been on my side, my faith would have crumbled, and I would never have been able to withstand the struggle I endured.

My friend, ministry is much the same way. Do you ever wonder, "Does God even hear me? Does He see the sacrifice we're making as a ministry family? Why does He allow the attacks to come, the hurtful words, and the discouragement to crush me?"

Does your heart cry out, desperate for an answer that seems as if it never comes? Cling to the truth of Psalm 124: "If it had not been the Lord on your side."

He hears, He listens, He knows, and He alone sustains you. Cry out to Him.

Amber Fox

Lord, You are on my side. Let me not forget that, even when You seem silent. In those times, may I seek to know You even more, to walk by faith, not by sight. Amen.

Behold, God is my salvation; I will trust, and will not be afraid; for the Lord God is my strength and my song, and he has become my salvation. With joy you will draw water from the wells of salvation.
Isaiah 12:2-3

"There are two ways to get enough. One is to continue to accumulate more and more. The other is to desire less."
G.K. Chesterton

The root of all joy is gratitude and contentment: **gratitude** because you realize how much you truly possess (namely things that cannot be bought), and **contentment** because you realize it is enough. Joy has to be sourced in something. In the case of a resurrected believer, our source is not *something* but *Someone*. God is the ultimate source of joy!

A deep-seated joy comes from a delight and personal knowledge of a God who is ultimately satisfying. Our hearts are so easily satisfied by little gods and amused by things that so easily distract us. These do not bring us true joy. True joy comes from delighting in and enjoying God.

I hate it when I snack before dinner, and then, when something delicious, nutritious, and more fully satisfying is set before me, I'm not hungry. In *A Hunger for God*, John Piper compares that to our desire for God: "If you don't feel strong desires for the manifestation of the glory of God, it is not because you have drunk deeply and are satisfied. It is because you have nibbled so long at the table of the world. Your soul is stuffed with small things, and there is no room for the great."

Joy is a serious business. Paul commands us to rejoice in the Lord **always**, and the psalmist cries out, "Let all who take refuge in you rejoice; let them sing joyful praises forever" (Psalm 5:11 NLT). Joy is not based on our circumstances but in trusting God as our refuge *in spite of* our circumstances. Joy gives us hope because we have been given an eternal lens through which to view our world. Joy comes from the belief that God is up to something good for us in all our delays and detours!

Chelsea Hall

"Let Thy goodness like a fetter bind my wandering heart to Thee. Prone to wander Lord, I feel it. Prone to leave the God I love; Here's my heart—O take and seal it, seal it for Thy courts above."
(from the hymn "Come Thou Fount of Every Blessing"
by Robert Robinson)

When the Lord restored the fortunes of Zion, we were like those who dreamed. Our mouths were filled with laughter, our tongues with songs of joy. Then it was said among the nations, "The Lord has done great things for them." The Lord has done great things for us, and we are filled with joy.

Psalm 126:1-3 NIV

$\mathcal{M}$y husband and I are not great at intentionally cultivating our marriage. We are more likely trading children around as we head to another meeting. We don't have date nights, and we are terrible at buying each other presents.

But I think we would both say we have a great marriage, and I think those who know us well would say the same. We try to have one thing, no matter our circumstances...

Laughter.

We love to laugh, and we both think of ourselves as one of the funniest people alive. We think we have more wit and charm than the average person. Fortunately, we find each other almost equally as humorous, witty, and charming.

We often get bogged down in the everyday tasks of ministry, and we are sometimes horrible at self-care and "couple-care." Yet we often find ourselves with joy in simple, everyday situations and thankful for the things that living in a small town allows.

We try to remember that a close-knit community is not a nuisance but a blessing, even if it is humorous as I run into the grocery store and meet every person I know while I attempt to get just one thing.

Building joy and laughter into our routine helps as well. Taking family walks to the town square, playing with our kids outside, and having church game nights allow us to have fun. Having our church see us this way benefits the relationships of everyone in the church. It shows our humanity and reminds the church that we are just a regular family.

The first half of Psalm 126 has an emphasis on joy and laughter and how it is a product of the Lord blessing the Israelites. They were so joyful and their mouths were filled with laughter, and everyone around them noticed.

My husband and I may not always take the time we should to work on our marriage, but giving ourselves time to spend together and to be filled with joy and laughter is the best way we know to relieve stress and to enjoy one another to the fullest. Laughter is also one way we can show the love of God to each other and those around us.

Cara Kipp

Lord, thank you for Your gift of laughter. Even when we face trials, we can find joy in Your provision. Help all of us to remember to have fun with others as we seek to serve and glorify You with our mouths and our actions. Amen.

Contribute to the needs of the saints and seek to show hospitality.
Romans 12:13

$\mathcal{A}$ few years ago, on the spur of the moment, a friend invited me to her home for lunch. She had the day off, and as she prepared her lunch, she wanted to share the meal with guests. A quick phone call and two of us set aside our plans for an even better plan.

We arrived at noon to a table set with chicken salad, pears and cottage cheese, ripe red tomato wedges, and tapioca pudding with raspberries — a delicious simple meal, made excellent by laughter and friendship.

We used everyday dishes and laughed that she'd put off her cleaning to prepare lunch — so once we left, she had to dive in to do all the cleaning that we didn't notice needed to be done.

While we often think of daintily set tables with sparkling china, silver, and crystal as the criteria for hospitality, it was my friend's joy in serving and being with us that made everything sparkle. Several times she remarked how glad she was that we could come. I'm not sure I've ever felt so welcomed, so wanted.

I still smile as I think of her enthusiasm of hospitality. Through her example, God reminded me of what hospitality is:

- Joy in serving
- Opening your home
- Encouraging
- Sharing together your joys and sorrows, your lives
- Laughing

- Thanking God for His blessings
- Being His blessing to others
- Forgetting yourself and glorifying Him

and what it is not:
- Having a perfectly clean home
- Having a perfectly decorated home
- Planning for weeks
- Preparing elaborate dishes
- Pulling out your best china
- Stressing over the details
- Wearing a frown

The joy on my friend's face will remain a very special memory as well as a reminder that God loves it when we offer hospitality. Romans 12:13 tells us to "practice hospitality" (NIV). We need to do it often! Remember, practice makes perfect. Hebrews 13:2 tells us to include strangers, not just our friends, in our hospitality. And 1 Peter 4:9 reminds us to be hospitable without complaining. (It's almost as if God knows us, isn't it?)

Lynnette Goebel

Heavenly Father, give us opportunities and passion to practice hospitality. Give us joy and use us to bring joy to others. Amen.

Rejoice in hope, be patient in tribulation, be constant in prayer.
Romans 12:12

*M*y husband and I enjoy being together, and one very important reason we have that joy is because we work hard at communicating and connecting with each other. We like to say we specialize in communication.

This can be challenging in busy ministry life! One obvious way to be intentional about this is through intentional date nights. A less obvious way is mentioned in Paul Tripp's book *What Did You Expect?* where he says, "The character and quality of our life is forged in **little moments**. Every day we lay little bricks on the foundation of what our life will be."

We can find joy through the little moments of connection with one another every day: a quick hug, a moment of laughter together, a short walk down the road, or even a moment of crying together. Grief and pain are not fun, but crying out to God with my husband *always* draws us closer together, bringing a sweet joy as we are constant in prayer (Romans 12:12).

Here are some simple ways I try to communicate well with my husband:
1. **Put the phone down**—I can make little moments count by putting my phone down and giving him my full attention.
2. **Touch base with him during the day**—I love sending him a quick text occasionally, asking how he's doing or just saying "I love you."
3. **Choose grace**—In the moments of frustration, I can choose grace by leaning on God's strength. The more often I am able to choose grace in those moments, the

more often I am able to "lay little bricks" that build something beautiful.

4. **Stay intimate** — This applies both physically and emotionally, especially because the two are connected. When we are feeling distant from each other, it's a reminder to reconnect.

5. **Study the Word together** — We don't have a particular schedule we stick to, but being able to discuss God's Word and what we're learning is a crucial part of our marriage.

6. **Pray together** — Praying together provides a depth of honesty and vulnerability that is necessary for real intimacy to take place, and I believe it is essential to a strong and healthy marriage.

What way can you focus on growing in your communication as a couple?

Tobi Henschel

Lord, thank You for my husband. Please help us to build little moments together so that we can be filled with joy in You! Amen.

Remember the Pain in the Joy 60

Looking to Jesus, the founder and perfecter of our faith, who for the joy that was set before him endured the cross, despising the shame, and is seated at the right hand of the throne of God.

Hebrews 12:2

*E*veryone always told me that when you hold your newborn in your arms for the first time, you forget all the pain required to bring her into the world. I was fortunate to be able to go home within twelve hours of the birth of our firstborn because she arrived too quickly for us to travel to the city where she was supposed to be born.

Since our doctor knew the nature of our curious small-town folk, he got us discharged as soon as possible. He gave my husband specific instructions: drop your wife and daughter off at the house, drive down the highway, park the car in a neighbor's driveway, and walk back home. He knew that people would start flocking in because news travels faster than the internet in a small town.

My husband didn't park the car down the road, but we tried to hide away for a time and enjoy the excitement of being new parents.

People still stopped by, so we had to tell the birth story over and over, and after I said goodbye to our guests and fed my baby again, I'd think back over the previous few hours and days. The problem was that when I remembered the pain, my mind recoiled from the recollection.

What was with this? They all said I wouldn't remember the pain! And I didn't want to — it hurt a lot, even the memory of it!

It doesn't mean the joy wasn't there, too, but every time my mind visited those hours that brought my daughter into the world, I had to push the pain out of my mind as it was too acute to think about.

To say we won't remember the pain isn't true, and I think Christ knew this, too. It says in this verse from Hebrews that He despised the shame. He certainly didn't enjoy the suffering and pain He endured for our sake, but His pain is still remembered because it is a part of the joy of giving us new birth.

I'm glad He doesn't forget His pain for our sake, aren't you?

Wendy McCready

Jesus, thank you for enduring the pain of my sin; let me not forget the pain that my sin cost You. Help me to see the joy in my current pain for Your glory. Amen.

Faithfulness

And let us not grow weary of doing good, for in due season we will reap, if we do not give up.

Galatians 6:9

*I*t is God who is faithful, and our biggest job is to believe that. It is His faithfulness that leads us to our own. Our faithfulness, however feeble it might be on any given day, is always a response to the love we have been shown.

This is very good news. We follow a good God who loves us very much. We are safe. That security releases us to trust God in ever-deepening ways and to step out in faithfulness in our own lives and churches.

As women married to pastors, we have a front-row seat to the gentle and powerful ways God works in the lives of the people who attend the churches our husbands serve. I've always thought that was one of the biggest perks of this life we live — to be able to hear the stories of God's mercies in the lives of the women and men we share our lives with and to watch their growing faith, which helps my faith. (That almost sounds a little bit selfish, but I do think it's a real core benefit.) It really is a privilege to be such a close witness to this wonder.

In this section of the devotional, we explore faithfulness — God's faithfulness to us and ours to Him. We can be faithful because He is faithful.

Karen Stiller

Trusting in God's Plan: 61
(Even When I Don't Understand It)

Trust in the LORD with all your heart, and do not lean on your own understanding. In all your ways acknowledge him, and he will make straight your paths.

Proverbs 3:5-6

I remember accepting Jesus as my Saviour when I knelt down at my bedside and asked Him into my heart. I suppose I was about six or seven years old, and my prayer was a simple child's prayer. I went downstairs and told my mom what I had done, but I did not know that it was the beginning of a journey that would lead me to become a pastor's wife.

I never dreamed of one day marrying and becoming a help-meet for a minister. In fact, I was raised in a denomination that did not have pastors. I had no concept whatsoever of what it meant to be a pastor's wife.

When we decided to get married, my husband was working as a sound technician. I had no inkling that he had ever felt a call to the ministry. God, however, had different plans for my husband and, ultimately, for me as well. As we grew closer together, he told me how, as a little boy, he had always wanted to be a minister, but as childhood dreams often do, that had fallen by the wayside in the face of more practical considerations.

Soon after we got married, he began to feel very strongly that God was calling him to be a minister. In order to prepare, he began to take online courses to obtain his B.A. in Christian Studies.

Eight years ago, when our minister got sick, it made sense for Gord to fill in for him. He asked Gord to "look after this little flock" during his absence. He never returned to preach full time, and Gord is still shepherding the flock. Suddenly, I was a pastor's wife.

Proverbs 3:5-6 tells us to place our trust in God rather than to rely on our own understanding. Often it is impossible to even conceive of the plans that God has in store for us. We can only trust in Him and put our faith in His goodness. God's plans are so much greater than ours and often well beyond our comprehension. When we trust Him and follow His leading, our lives will be richly blessed, often in surprising and wonderful ways.

Marcy Ardis

Dear Lord, thank You for the plans You have put in place for my life. You have richly blessed my family and me through Your kindness, mercy, grace, and love. Remind me to place my trust in You each day of my life. Amen.

He must increase, but I must decrease.

John 3:30

Every day I live under this persistent condition—I am helpless. Unable to change hearts. Incapable of controlling circumstances. Weak instead of strong.

Every day I am helpless, but I hang onto the perception of what I believe I can change and control. I think it's especially persistent among us pastors' wives. For every pastor's wife who seems to have no concept of how her tongue and actions can affect her husband's ministry, I think there are one hundred more of us who feel we are capable of more than we actually are.

I see this ministry syndrome mirrored in the life of Elijah in 1 Kings 19. Elijah has fled for his life from Jezebel. God comes near to him and asks what he is doing. Elijah replies, "The people of Israel have forsaken your covenant, thrown down your altars, and killed your prophets with the sword, and I, even I only, am left, and they seek my life, to take it away" (1 Kings 19:10). Do you see the essence of what Elijah is saying? Basically, "I am the ministry lynchpin, and it all depends on me."

And how does God answer Elijah? "I will leave seven thousand in Israel, all the knees that have not bowed to Baal" (I Kings 19:18). All along, God was working in a much bigger way than Elijah could see. When we've been believing that it all depends on us, it's startling to realize that we are just a tiny player in the grand scheme of God's great work. It's humbling and freeing and *hard*.

So where does that leave me? It reduces me to prayer. And why, *why does that not feel like enough?* Why would I think my work could be greater than inviting God to work? I think I have finally figured this out — my greatest ministry, whether we are talking about the church or my family, will always be prayer. Nobody knows the church quite like my husband and I do, and nobody knows the pastor quite like I do, so nobody can pray like I can pray. *This is my first calling.* I want to fix, comfort, and encourage — God wants me first to kneel.

Sarah Johnson

Lord, may my view of self be small and my view of You be large, and may the end result be a life of prayerful dependence on You. Today, let my first ministry be prayer. Amen.

Or do you presume on the riches of his kindness and forbearance and patience, not knowing that God's kindness is meant to lead you to repentance?

Romans 2:4

$\mathcal{H}$ave you ever been embarrassed at church by your kids because "pastors' kids should know better"? Here's the secret about pastors' kids (PKs) — they're just kids. They, like all of us, are people made in God's image and sinners in need of God's grace. Here are three things I've learned about raising PKs:

1. Have grace. My kids are going to mess up and need correction and guidance. In His infinite wisdom, God bestows grace, kindness, and patience on me as His child, so this is the example I have for how to correct my children. When they sin, I need to lovingly and firmly point them to the truth of Scripture without shaming them for their actions or bringing up their status as a PK to scold them.

2. Give them freedom to be kids. People sometimes unfairly extend the calling of the pastor onto his children, placing extrabiblical expectations on them. But the kids haven't been called into ministry — their father has. It isn't their job to minister to the church body — it's their dad's job.

As we raise PKs, it is right to expect obedience, as that is their job as our children (Ephesians 6:1). However, we should not expect our kids to be "mini pastors," whatever that might look like. When we are tempted to yield to extra-Biblical expectations, it is helpful to remember that we answer to God for our parenting, not to other people.

3. Foster heart over performance. While there's nothing wrong with being happy about our children doing well and wanting to encourage them, we need to be careful not to become obsessed with how they perform. For example, my son could say 20 Bible verses about showing kindness to others but then turn around and yell at his brother. If I simply praise his Bible memorization but don't address the lack of kindness in his heart, what has he learned? We need to be more concerned about the state of our children's hearts and less about their outward appearance or performance (1 Samuel 16:7).

Which of these areas of parenting do you see as a strength in your household? As a weakness? Ask God for His help today!

Tobi Henschel

Lord, please guide us as parents. Fill us with Your grace as we raise these children, that they might be led to true repentance and a life dedicated to You. Amen.

Faithful to Rest: 64
A Pastoral Couple's Achilles' Heel

The Lord is my shepherd; I shall not want. He makes me lie down in green pastures. He leads me beside still waters. He restores my soul.
Psalm 23:1-3a

*N*ew to ministry, I remember sitting in a seminar room with other pastors' wives when our speaker asked us to write down one ministry fear. I surprised myself by writing "to be too tired to serve well." I feared burnout!

Almost two decades later, my propensity is still toward burning the candle at both ends, but my soul has a greater awareness and longing to find my rest in God's faithfulness. Is the idea of ministry rest an Achilles' heel for you, too?

I see spiritual similarities from a Google word study: "An Achilles' heel is a weakness in spite of an overall strength which can lead to downfall. Symptoms include pain and limited range of motion. The cure? Rest, support, and flexing exercises for the ankles. Left untreated? Painful rupture of the tendons and inability to move fully." Rest is crucial for our bodies physically, just as times of respite are needed for longevity in ministry.

Lois Seadore, a friend and a pastor's wife of over forty years, says, "Biblical rest is an attitude of *heart* that directly relates to weariness of the soul which in turn affects the *body*." Resting in the Lord becomes reality as we let God be our sole support: our Rock, Refuge, and Strength.

God gives restful advice to the Israelites, and they respond negatively, "Thus says the LORD: 'Stand by the roads, and look, and ask for the ancient paths, where the good way is;

and walk in it, and find rest for your souls.' But they said, 'We will not walk in it'" (Jeremiah 6:16).

There are three ways we as pastoral couples can find rest for our souls:

1. **Soulful and Creative Rest**—resting in God's Word, in prayer, in worship, in nature, in creativity
2. **Family Rest**—regularly taking time to enjoy life as a family (outside of ministry)
3. **Friendship Rest**—rejuvenating by spending time with friends

Psalm 23 describes one of the most "restful" pictures in the history of mankind. If we let our culture shepherd us, there will be no rest; as we let God and His Word shepherd us, we find green pastures and quiet waters for our weary souls. Read this passage tonight before falling asleep!

Denna Busenitz

Lord God, lead me beside still waters and restore my soul through Your gift of rest. Amen.

For your Maker is your husband, the LORD of hosts is his name; and the Holy One of Israel is your Redeemer, the God of the whole earth he is called.

Isaiah 54:5

I will never forget my introduction to a lady in the first church my husband and I served as a young married couple. I was doing my pastor's wife thing, chatting with people during the coffee time. I hadn't met this lady yet, so I began by introducing myself. "Hi, I'm Wendy, Mark the pastor's wife." She grinned, revealing bright white teeth in a gorgeous and open smile. Right away I felt at ease, until she responded to my introduction not by offering her first name, but by saying, "Oh…you're the one whose job it is to seduce the pastor!"

Initially I was inwardly shocked at her statement, but I confess I've been blessed by the wisdom of it. I've learned that the best ministry-marriage protection is to make my marriage a priority and not give my husband any reason to go looking anywhere else.

We can have a faithful marriage if we fortify our marriage by putting guards in place.

A number of times men in our congregation have approached me regularly for conversation, and I have had that uncomfortable feeling that something isn't right. We need to trust those instincts.

We also need to not place ourselves in a position where we are alone with a member of the opposite sex. Those are guards that fortify our marriages.

We must unite to make our husbands a priority. Take time to invest in your relationship with him by serving him in love for the unique person he is. This will unite you and give fullness to your relationship.

But what if my husband begins to show a lack of interest in me even if I do all these things? What if he's preoccupied with ministry stresses or is unwell or depressed? Some of these troubles may be a direct result of your husband's sin, and we shouldn't take those sins on ourselves; Jesus already did.

In the meantime, we also need to love our God first and foremost. When I'm tempted to be peeved at my husband's lack, I have to remember that only God will meet my needs; HE is the Lover of my soul, and my deepest longings for intimacy will only be met ultimately in Him.

Finally, we must leave our marriages in God's hands. Prayer will unite us as one and give us what we need to love God first and then each other, and can bring healing and restoration when we have failed.

Wendy McCready

Lord, You are my true Husband. Make my marriage a faithful reflection of Christ and His Church so that others will want to know Him. Amen.

And God is able to make all grace abound to you, so that having all sufficiency in all things at all times, you may abound in every good work.

2 Corinthians 9:8

This verse is posted in my kitchen window as a daily reminder to rely on God's grace and not on my own strength. I need His strength every minute of every day in order to walk in the Spirit and not in my flesh.

I have three kids (ages nine, six, and two), and I homeschool the older two. We are also doing foster care for a baby girl. There are many times a day when I just want some quiet time and my own space. I have many things that I want to accomplish and a list of things I need to get done. But every day, "It is His strength that gives us what we need in order to nurture life in the face of death and through a million deaths-to-self each day" (*The Pastor's Wife* by Gloria Furman, p. 11).

A mother and pastor's wife gives of herself every day, often from a place of emptiness. But God does not give us hypothetical grace for a hypothetical future, nor for hypothetical situations. He gives us abundant grace for each moment so that we may abound in every good work. Abundance means thriving in every season and situation, not merely surviving.

So, I will be fully present in each moment with my children and not see them as interruptions. I will be fully present with the woman after church who wants to have a longer conversation. I will be fully present with the Lord in each moment as He is working out my salvation so that Christ is formed in me (Philippians 2:12; Galatians 4:19).

Chelsea Hall

Thank you, Lord, that You give us exactly what we need each day, our daily bread. We look to You, our Supplier and Provider, just as the Israelites waited with hope and expectation each day that You would provide manna from Heaven. Amen.

And they sang a new song, saying, "Worthy are you to take the scroll and to open its seals, for you were slain, and by your blood you ransomed people for God from every tribe and language and people and nation."

Revelation 5:9

I've been playing the piano for most of my life. Way before my feet could reach the pedals, my fingers loved to press the keys, bringing music to my imaginative stories. Butterflies, clouds, and birds fluttered through my mind when I played the high keys, while trolls, monsters, and thunderstorms serenaded from the low keys. Years later, lessons began and I learned the theory, techniques, and passion of music.

The impact of music is powerful. When my dad succumbed to Alzheimer's Disease to the point where he no longer knew his family, he still remembered music. One day a local church held a service for the residents where he lived. As we sang "The Old Rugged Cross," Mom saw tears running down Dad's cheeks. He remembered the power of the cross through the power of music.

I find it amazing how music can bring memories swiftly to my mind—Mom singing old songs as she worked, hymns shared as favorites, a special song learned at camp.

"In the Garden" reminds me of Jo. Years ago, Jo came to me after the service and thanked me for playing it during the offering. She explained that it was the song playing the day she walked down the aisle and gave her life to Jesus. The song had opened the floodgates of memories from that day long ago. It encouraged her and gave her renewed hope.

On Sundays I love to sing with my church family, raising our voices together in praise to our great God, in love and worship, joy and lament.

Music. A blessing from the Creator. A gift we too often take for granted. Music is not an invention of man. The morning stars sang together as God laid the foundations of the earth (Job 38:7). The mountains, heavens, and earth will rejoice with singing one day (Isaiah 49:13), and God Himself will rejoice over us with singing (Zephaniah 3:17).

Lift your voice in praise today. To the Creator. To the Savior. To the Almighty God. Sing the old hymns. Remember His faithfulness. Sing new songs — for He continues to do marvelous things. And wait for the day when we will forever praise Him with joy and music.

Lynnette Goebel

Heavenly Father, how we thank You for the gift of music! May our lives today be filled with Your praises. Bring songs to our lips that we may continually praise Your name. Amen.

For the LORD God is a sun and shield; the LORD bestows favor and honor. No good thing does he withhold from those who walk uprightly. O LORD of hosts, blessed is the one who trusts in you!
                                        Psalm 84:11-12

*I*n May, school started to wrap up for my children, and friends started talking about summer vacation plans. In a desperate tone, I said to my husband, "I could really use a vacation." A particularly hard autumn rolled into an even more complicated winter, moving into a hectic spring with no end in sight. As a ministry family, we take our family vacation at odd times, choosing autumn as a time to get away.

As it often happens, I was convicted by one of my husband's sermons too late to keep my tongue in check. The message was on Psalm 84, and it struck close to my sin and my heart, and the end particularly fortified me.

God gives us all good things. He does not keep anything good from us. He doesn't give us too much or too little, just the perfect amount. When I feel my strength is failing, He gives me that, too (v. 5). I felt convicted to reflect on the blessings He had bestowed upon me instead of to dwell on the hard things that had come to pass.

The Lord had been our shield and kept my family safe through situations that could have brought harm. We had seen little miracles happen in our household and our ministry.

He allowed a wayward youth to rededicate her life to Him and be baptized. He guided me to a doctor who aided me in atypical symptoms I was having. He developed and strengthened important relationships within our church and with other families in ministry.

I often remember putting my feet on the floor on those mornings, feeling haggard, and my heart would whisper, "Today, Lord, You have to come through, because I just can't." Again and again, the Lord did. He came through, fortified, and protected.

At the time it felt like a bitter, desperate prayer but looking back, it feels more honest and trusting, and blessings flowed from it. The Lord heard my prayer as I stayed the difficult course He set before me, and, as always, it was worth it.

Cara Kipp

Lord, we know that You give abundantly and always give the perfect amount of what we need. Help us to remember that in times of trial, weariness, and hard-heartedness. Amen.

Brothers, pray for us.

1 Thessalonians 5:25

$\mathcal{A}$ good friend of mine, a former military wife, taught me about OPSEC—Operations Security. This is my basic understanding of OPSEC: within the military, critical details about operations cannot be shared in order to protect our troops. This means family members often don't know details about what their loved one is doing, or even if they do know, they cannot share those details with others. Military families often offer support and encouragement to one another, however, without needing to know any details, knowing that whatever is happening falls under the umbrella of OPSEC.

My friend has invited me to let her know when I need "OPSEC prayer." In other words, on days when ministry is especially difficult, when things are happening at our church which I cannot share, when my husband or my family has been hurt but I can't explain it, or any similar circumstance, I can simply text her and ask for OPSEC prayer. She will know that we need ministry prayer, respect the fact that I can't share any details, and pray for us.

Sometimes it can be hard to ask for prayer, especially when you can't explain why you need prayer, but we know it is Biblical to ask for prayer. The Apostle Paul asked for prayer in his letters many times. Some requests were for boldly proclaiming the gospel (Ephesians 6:19), God to open doors (Colossians 4:3), speaking clearly (Colossians 4:4), deliverance from wicked men (2 Thessalonians 3:2), and more.

Perhaps my favorite request of Paul's is in I Thessalonians 5:25, *"Brothers, pray for us."* Paul didn't unpack the "what" or "why". He simply told the Thessalonians to pray.

When we ask others to pray for us or when we pray for others, we are bearing one another's burdens. This is an important part of the family of Christ. We need to have people we trust and can turn to for OPSEC prayer, and we also need to be safe people for others to turn to in that same way.

Who are your OPSEC prayer partners, or whom can you ask to become partners with? How can you bear one another's burdens today?

Tobi Henschel

Father, please show me the people in my life I can ask to pray for me in this way. Help me to be an OPSEC prayer partner to the people around me. Amen.

Faithfulness in Suffering *70*

Therefore let those who suffer according to God's will entrust their souls to a faithful Creator while doing good.

1 Peter 4:19

*M*y husband and I read a book together called *The Basket of Flowers*, written in 1768 by Christoph von Schmid. The story tells of hardships and trials that fall upon a devout Christian widower who instructs his young daughter to look to the Lord who is her faithful Protector and Guide. Once again, I was reminded how God allows and also uses trials and unexplainable suffering — somehow — for His glory and our good.

While reading, I found myself reflecting on my relationship with my Heavenly Father and with my earthly father who passed away 10 years previously. There is comfort for me in knowing that what I missed with my earthly father, I have every opportunity to learn from my Heavenly Father.

As a 16-year-old, when I heard the news of Dad's tragic death, God's faithfulness flashed through my mind like a split-second movie. In those moments my subconscience was aware of my options to turn to academics, friends, money, etc., for comfort. Yet I knew that God was the only One who would give me the peace and joy I needed. Why? He had proved Himself faithful. And He would continue to be faithful.
This memory is a milestone experience for me of God's faithfulness alive in my life. God had answered my prayers by giving me what I asked for: Himself.

The various trials we face in our homes and ministries are opportunities for testing and growing our faith. In turn, our faith impacts our perseverance, holiness, and faithfulness, as James writes in chapter one.

The struggles of a pastor's wife have some different temptations than those of a teenage girl. In the shock or pain of suffering, you may be drawn to escape to perfectionism, your kids, your job, material wealth or personal interests. Unfortunately, on this earth suffering and trials are far from hypothetical. With each challenge comes a fork in the road where we must make a choice. Will we run from God? Or will we pursue our faithful Father with the faith He provides us?

Nicole Martin

Lord, in my present and future suffering, may I recall Your bountiful faithfulness towards me. I entrust my soul to You and ask for help that the trials I face might produce more faithfulness in me. Amen.

This is my commandment, that you love one another as I have loved you. Greater love has no one than this, that someone lay down his life for his friends.

John 15:12-13

*W*ith all of the social media out there you'd think that, as Christians, we'd be really good at loving each other. Why? Because Jesus told us that we should love our neighbor as we love ourselves.

We love ourselves pretty well, don't we? I mean, look at how often we post pictures of ourselves and our family members, what we had for breakfast, what we think, what we do, what we feel...for everyone to see.

Yikes! And yet...our churches are not overflowing with people?

In John 13, when Jesus gave the new commandment to His disciples that they should love one another, He explained why they should do this (John 13:34-35). It was so that the world would know that they were His disciples.

So...why don't people know that we are His disciples if we know how to love ourselves so well? Apparently, the way we love ourselves hasn't transferred to how we love one another. Our problem is that we haven't switched our focus from caring about ourselves to giving that same care and attention to loving the people around us.

Jesus wasn't plastering Him image for the whole world to see what He was doing. He wasn't about loving Himself, though He had every reason to, being God. That wasn't His way or

His plan. He could only do the will of His Father, and He submitted to that willingly, which required that He lay aside His glory and serve. Which He did. He washed His disciples' stinky feet.

Our feet aren't that pretty. We all have warts and calluses and dry skin and curled toenails with grime embedded underneath…until we clean them. Why do we do that? Because we love ourselves. We take care of our bodies because we care about ourselves.

And if we follow Jesus, we should care about our fellow neighbors (believers and unbelievers alike) enough to get down on our knees and wash their stinky feet. If we do this as followers of Jesus, then the world will know we are His disciples.

Maybe it's time I buy a foot bath.

Wendy McCready

Lord, I confess that loving others doesn't come naturally to me. Give me Your power to serve and love others faithfully. Amen.

For the whole law is fulfilled in one word: "You shall love your neighbor as yourself." But if you bite and devour one another, watch out that you are not consumed by one another.

Galatians 5:14-15

*I*f you attend a rural/small-town church like I do, you've been to a few potlucks. They seem to be a vanishing tradition in our days of instant-everything-crazy-fast-paced-two-income-earning households, but where we live, every fifth Sunday is always potluck Sunday. Everyone seems to enjoy trying his luck at the pot as he lines up, hoping that his favorite dish isn't gone when he reaches the front of the line.

My pastor-husband and I are often busy chatting with people after the service and occupied with caring for other things, so we tend to wait until everyone has gone through the line. There are times when the food has been hit pretty hard, and when it's our turn, the spread has been nearly demolished.

All that food has been bitten, devoured, consumed—gone! (It's a good thing our kitchen people don't bring the dessert out at the same time as the rest of the food!)

These verses from Galatians 5 are key for summarizing what it does and doesn't mean to love one another in the Body of Christ. We need to love one another, and that means we need to heed the warning in this passage—if you don't love your neighbor as yourself but instead choose to bite and devour each other, you will be consumed by one another.

I am afraid sometimes that our potlucks illustrate how we treat each other in the Body of Christ. Everyone tries to be the first in the line; everyone picks his favorite things and scrapes the bowl clean, devouring every last bite until it's all consumed, done, destroyed, with only a pile of dirty dishes left to wash up.

Instead of humbly serving one another with encouragement, kindness, and forgiveness, which build each other up, we are puffed up with judgment, envy, complaints, and anger, which all serve to tear each other down.

Now…I'm not against potlucks. I want to keep having them, but I hope that my life and the lives of the people in my church are not known for devouring each other like the food at the potlucks, but for humbly serving one another in love.

Anyone have a dishrag?

Wendy McCready

Jesus, You served others, and You never complained about it. I don't want to be one who bites and devours others with the words I say. Let me love and serve You by serving others. Amen.

Faithful in Prayer: 73
A Tribute to Pastors Everywhere

And the prayer of faith will save the one who is sick, and the Lord will raise him up. And if he has committed sins, he will be forgiven. Therefore, confess your sins to one another and pray for one another, that you may be healed. The prayer of a righteous person has great power as it is working.

James 5:15-16

I see a lot of statistics on pastors these days; many are shocking, sobering, or discouraging. And I get it. As a rural church-planter's wife, I've seen the toll of ministry labor on my husband. But I've also witnessed firsthand how God answers the earnest prayers of my shepherd-husband.

What might the prayer statistics for pastors around the world look like? Prayers of faith are being voiced during crises, fiery trials, awesome spiritual revivals, when others are ill, when things look hopeless. The power isn't in the position of a pastor; it's in the prayers of a righteous person.

I was cleaning my husband's office several months ago and found his personal prayer sheet tucked in his Bible. I was moved to tears as I read names and requests that my husband prays for as he's alone with the Lord. Pray for your pastor to keep praying daily prayers of faith; it matters!

How about pastors around the world — what are their prayers of faith for?
- Courage to pastor their flocks regardless of prison/death threats
- Wisdom to preach the Word on all occasions
- Love and forgiveness for people, especially those who insult and revile them

- Support financially and prayerfully to provide for their families and continue pastoring
- Strength to focus on evangelism and discipleship
- Peace in their homes, churches, and communities

Moms in Prayer International President, Sally Burke, reminds us that corporate prayer is the most mentioned type of prayer in the Bible. Support your pastors' attendance at gatherings (locally, online, traveling) where they will have a chance to pray prayers of faith with other pastors. It just might change the statistics.

Denna Busenitz

Lord God, I pray for pastors around the world to persevere with prayers of faith. Amen.

The heart is deceitful above all things, and desperately sick; who can understand it?

Jeremiah 17:9

$\mathcal{T}$urn on the news these days, and accusations are flying. People are positive someone did something with the worst of motives. They know this person is lying. They did it. They meant to do it. And we know why.

In her book *None Like Him*, Jen Wilkins reminds us that God is incomprehensible. He alone fully knows Himself. Unlike Him, we cannot fully know ourselves, let alone others.

Romans 11:33 describes our incomprehensible God. The Infinite who cannot be fully known by the finite. *"Oh, the depth of the riches and wisdom and knowledge of God! How unsearchable are his judgments and how inscrutable his ways!"*

"Such knowledge [of God] should cause me to worship. The depths of the riches and wisdom and knowledge of God should bring me to my knees. His unsearchable judgments and inscrutable ways should inspire right reverence. And the glorious fact that he makes himself known in ways my finite understanding can grasp should cause me to celebrate, to devote my life to the joyful duty of discovering what he has made known of himself." (*None Like Him*, p. 39)

We finite human beings, created by the uncreated God, have it all wrong. We think we know everything. But we do not. We know God by what He has revealed to us in His Word and in His creation. But we forget who He is and think we are much greater than we are.

Ah, pride. It so easily besets us. When I should be on my knees, I'm judging my sister's motives. When I should be worshiping my Creator, I'm criticizing my friends. When I should be honoring Almighty God, I'm hurting His church.

But when we meditate on Who He is, we realize just how small we are. His love says we are valuable. His Being reminds us we are His. We must change our actions and thoughts to bring them in line with the Truth.

Do you sometimes slip into forgetfulness like I do? Have you acted more like you are God than you are His child? Judged someone unfairly? Acted superior?

Let's get back to remembering God and falling on our knees.

Let's honor Him with our words, thoughts, and actions.

Let's celebrate what He has shown us and devote our lives to learning more about Him!

Lynnette Goebel

Heavenly Father, we praise and celebrate You because You are the Only God—Almighty and Holy. You are so much more than we can comprehend. Open our eyes, Father, and reveal Yourself to us each day. May we see You at work in us today. Help us to honor You today and every day. Amen.

Then he said to Thomas, "Put your finger here, and see my hands; and put out your hand, and place it in my side. Do not disbelieve, but believe." Thomas answered him, "My Lord and my God!"
John 20:27-28

*T*homas is the name of our youngest son. We named him after the disciple in the Bible who said he wouldn't believe Jesus was alive until he could see and touch Jesus' wounds for himself. Our son's middle name is Jacob. When my husband's grandmother, a minister's wife and widow, met her great-grandson, she said, "That is a very big name for a little baby."

She was probably right. We combined two great Biblical stories of men of faith into one heavy handle for our little guy. We loved that Thomas the disciple dared to say his doubt out loud and grew because of it. He had courage to ask and admit it, there in the midst of the others who all believed more than he did — or appeared to. Their stronger faith didn't intimidate him. His demand for proof would have helped everybody. It helps us today to just read about it.

That's what being honest almost always does. It helps everybody.

I have found this to be true in my life as a minister's wife. My own doubts — and willingness to *wrestle* with them — helps to heal them, to make them less powerful and frightening for me and also for others. Don't get me wrong. I don't go around sharing out loud every time I have a nagging thought about faith or God and His Church that is not healthy or helpful.

But I am willing, especially in the special moments of intimacy in a women's Bible study or coffee with a friend, to confess that the woman married to the minister is not a spiritual superhero, and that we all have times of doubt, struggling, and maybe even feelings of estrangement from God. It helps me, and it helps my friend when I say it out loud.

Normalizing doubt removes its weight and worry. We aren't terrible people after all. We are humans with questions who wrestle with mystery. It's okay. The Biblical account, especially those tender moments between Thomas and the newly risen Jesus, shows that doubt is real and normal and not an obstacle to belief after all, but a bridge to deeper belief. When confessed, doubt is an opportunity for God to show His faithfulness to us and to others. What a relief!

Karen Stiller

Dear God, You stood before Thomas and said, "Touch and see." I join with him today in proclaiming you my Lord and my God. Give me strength to be honest with my doubts so I can be strong in my faith. Amen.

He Is Not Slow   76

The Lord is not slow to fulfill his promise as some count slowness, but is patient toward you, not wishing that any should perish, but that all should reach repentance.

2 Peter 3:9

One of the joys of ministry is seeing people come to know Christ: to see the light of Christ shining in their lives for the first time and to see sheep who were wandering enter the fold. Then there are those you are cheering for, but it seems it's always one step forward, two steps back. You pray, you reach out, and disappointment sets in.

But God. Don't you love those two words? God is faithful. He is not slow. He is working. We pray and we wait for what seems like an eternity. We wait for the rebel to repent, for the wayward child to return home, and for the broken to be reconciled. We wait impatiently, but God is patient and He is not slow.

We were having dinner with a godly, older couple from our church recently. While listening to their faith stories, the husband shared that he had walked away from the Lord for a decade or so. A decade?! Even as a 40-year-old who has been in ministry for the last 14 years, a decade seems so long to me. In the midst of the waiting, it feels slow, but the Lord is not slow, and His timing is truly perfect.

So, let us pray. Let us faithfully reach out to those who are broken, those who are hurting, and those who are wayward. Let us trust in "Him who is able to do far more abundantly than all that we ask or think" (Ephesians 3:20).

Jennifer McConnell

Heavenly Father, we thank You that You are not slow in fulfilling Your promises, that Your timing is always perfect, and that Your plans cannot be thwarted. Help us to be faithful and to be prayerful in all things and to trust You with the results. May You receive all the glory and praise for Your work in Your people. Amen.

*And which of you by being anxious can add a single hour to his span
of life? If then you are not able to do as small a thing as that, why
are you anxious about the rest?*

Luke 12:25-26

*R*ecently, there was a stressful situation coming to a head for
us, one which I had spent much time praying over. On that
important morning, I had a moment of panic and thought,
"Oh no, I haven't spent enough time thinking about this!"
Now, let's translate that deep and spiritual thought — what I
really meant was, "Oh no, I didn't worry enough!" Ludicrous,
right?

I used to scoff a bit when reading Jesus' words about worry
in Luke 12 — who would actually think he could make his life
longer simply by worrying about it?

But on that morning, I realized *I* am that person. That crazy
thought that I entertained for a mere second opened my eyes.
I may say with my lips that I know worrying is pointless, but
I still do it. I still think that I, in my humanness, can change
the outcome of a decision simply by worrying about it.

Instead of wasting my time worrying, I need to actually *do*
what I know I need to do — keep handing it over to God. Every
time that worrisome thought comes to mind, I pray about it.
However, I don't just ask God to fix it. I fix my eyes on Him,
the Founder and Perfecter of my faith (Hebrews 12:2).
I remember Who He is, and then I hand the worry over to
Him. I ask Him to do His will and ask for His strength to sustain me throughout the worry. Then — I leave it with Him.

I don't keep taking the worry back so I can stew over it. I leave it there. In His hands. And every time the worry pops back into my mind, I do the whole process over again: Remember Him. Hand it over to Him. Ask for His help. Leave it there. Again. I do this as often as I need to until the worry is no longer a worry.

When I do this, I truly find God's peace described in Philippians 4:6-7. What are you worrying about today? Take a moment to pray over it and hand it over to God and leave it with Him.

Tobi Henschel

Father, help me to trust You with my worries. Help me to leave them in Your hands and remember instead Who You are and what You have done for me. Amen.

The Lord is my shepherd; I shall not want. He makes me lie down in green pastures. He leads me beside still waters. He restores my soul.
Psalm 23:1-3a

I have a bad habit of tucking broken things into drawers. I often don't have the time or desire to deal with things when they break, and I don't want to look at them lying around, so I shut them up in drawers. Then, when I am looking for something, I open up a drawer and find little bits and pieces of things that were once lovely and whole but are now just shards of their former loveliness. Oh, I might think about them and wish I had time to fix them, but I usually don't fix them. I never find a lot of time to dwell on the things that have been broken in the past.

A forced slowdown required my priorities to change. Suddenly, I was at home every day, and, while life was busy, it was also slower and quieter. I opened up a drawer and found some broken toys and, instead of shutting them up in the drawer again, I pulled them out and lined them up for my husband to fix.

As I was lining up the broken parts to be fixed, I was hit with an idea that resonated right through me. Just as these toys could not get fixed until life quieted down around us, so too, I cannot be fixed until I rest in the quietness of God's peace that we have through His great love and mercy.

The NIV translation of Psalm 23:3 says "He leads me beside quiet waters." It is when we experience quiet in our lives that we begin to feel the healing touch of God's grace.

True restoration begins when we take the time to lie quietly in the green pastures located beside the still waters. It begins when we acknowledge how truly broken we are.

We all need God's restoration. We are all missing parts that only He can replace. Instead of reaching out to our loving Father in our brokenness, we often hide ourselves away, just like I tucked all the broken pieces away in drawers. When we recognize our brokenness and hurt and sit in the stillness and peace which only God can offer, He takes the shards of our shattered lives and makes us whole again.

Marcy Ardis

Dear Lord, help me to be still and to sit in quietness in Your presence. I offer my brokenness up to You. Heal me and use me for Your purposes today. Amen.

Where shall I go from your Spirit? Or where shall I flee from your presence? If I ascend to heaven, you are there! If I make my bed in Sheol, you are there! If I take the wings of the morning and dwell in the uttermost parts of the sea, even there your hand shall lead me, and your right hand shall hold me.

Psalm 139:7-10

*A*nxiety in our world is at an all-time high. Yet, for the pastor's wife the anxieties don't stop there. How can we help our people face difficult times? How do we maintain unity? What if we are just not enough? You might be the only ministry couple at your church. How do you work through the anxieties of the world and then combine that with the regular struggles of the ministry?

Anxiety is a part of life for all of us. At some level, each person has to deal with it. In my own life it has been a constant battle. As a child of God, a mother, a friend, and a pastor's wife, anxieties come in waves which overwhelm me, taking my breath away and seemingly tossing me to and fro until I'm thrown to the sand, exhausted and bruised. It is a battleground trodden down through unwelcome repetition.

However, it is through these stormy waves of anxiety that God's hope shines ever brighter. I have learned, through His pursuit of me, to rely on Him as the faithful Rescuer.
He uses His Word and the Holy Spirit to toss me a life ring, tethering me to His promises and bringing peace and safety in the midst of the fear. And it is in this rescue that I find the ability to obey His words: "Be anxious for nothing" (Philippians 4:6).

To build confidence in this trust, Psalm 139 guides us into the surety we can have in God's promised omnipresence. The psalmist begins and ends this beautiful passage by explaining how intimately God knows each of us. Just the knowledge that He understands so well should provide a calm assurance.

Yet He doesn't stop there. Did you see all those *if* phrases in our Psalms passage? From the darkest depth to the highest height, there is no worry, no fear, no anxiety in which God will not be with us! We must only look to our Rescuer to weather the storm.

What are your anxieties today, dear friend? Remember, even *if*...God is there. Tether yourself to your omnipresent, ever-loving Rescuer. He is faithful.

Sarah Chadbourn

Oh, Lord, my burdened heart cries out to You. Yet even as I feel overwhelmed by sorrow, I will choose to cling to You, my Hope and my Salvation. I choose today to trust in my Rescuer. Amen.

Blessed be the God and Father of our Lord Jesus Christ! According to his great mercy, he has caused us to be born again to a living hope through the resurrection of Jesus Christ from the dead, to an inheritance that is imperishable, undefiled, and unfading, kept in heaven for you.

1 Peter 1:3-4

$\mathcal{A}$s I looked around my yard and flowerbeds at the end of winter, I was so discouraged. Remnants of dead leaves and acorns from last fall lay scattered all over the ground. As I began to rake the stalks, sticks, and shreds into piles, I uncovered life beginning to sprout underneath. With determination, my daffodils, irises, and crocuses were sprouting up through my unkempt yard. I had done nothing to coax them, but they were firm and hardy little plants.

Everything in this broken world echoes in our hearts that this is not how things were meant to be. My garden is a far cry from the Garden of Eden, and my heart longs for that kind of beauty and perfection. The opposite of the heavenly inheritance that awaits me, my garden is perishable, defiled, and fading.

Like a gardener, God is faithful to prune the areas of my life that are unwieldy and to resurrect the parts of me that are dead. Spring reminds us that He is faithful to keep His promises and that we can have a confident hope in resurrection life.

My husband and I are beginning our journey into the world of foster care and adoption. I have sat with several friends in tears as they have to "give their kids back" in the reunification process.

I anticipate that this attachment and loss will be the most painful thing for me. I often feel that loving that deeply will cost me, and my first instinct is the self-preservation of hardening my heart. However, I feel the Holy Spirit nudging me to keep my heart open and to love hard and deeply even at the risk of getting hurt.

God works through loss to protect our hearts from giving our worship to lesser things. People disappoint us, our bodies age and grow weak, flowers die, and food becomes an enemy. All of these things are designed to deepen our love and worship of Him. He is completing the good work that He started in us, so, my dear sister, trust His faithfulness to be a good Surgeon of your heart, and let Him mature you through each trial!

Chelsea Hall

Lord, I know in my heart that this world is not how things were meant to be. I put my hope in You to satisfy my longings. Amen.

*Praying at all times in the Spirit, with all prayer and supplication.
To that end, keep alert with all perseverance, making supplication
for all the saints.*

Ephesians 6:18

I recently heard someone make a comment about "Mrs. Job"
in reference to a previous pastor's wife who called to share a
prayer request. It seems that for the past several years this
pastoral couple had been besieged by many health issues and
subsequent financial and emotional needs, and they had
called the church many times to ask for prayer support.

This was not my pastor and wife, nor do I know people in that
church. I'm sure that many are faithfully praying for this couple. At one point, someone probably made the comment that
they must feel like Job and his wife as so many things seemed
to be coming at them one right after the other. And the nick-
name "Mrs. Job" stuck.

I've had some health issues in the past, and I've depended on
my church family to pray me through them. One time I hurt
my knee, and this comment about Mrs. Job came to mind. I
thought, "What will people think if I ask for prayer *again?*"

I almost didn't ask for help because I was afraid of what people might think. It was pride rearing its ugly head. Although
I'm pretty sure they would have noticed me walking around
on crutches, my first thought was to handle it by myself.

I think all of us have fallen into this trap at one time or another. We don't want to bother people. We wonder what they
will think. We are afraid to show our weakness. We want to
keep things private.

But God has given us the *privilege* to pray for one another as well as for ourselves. Read through Paul's letters, and you will see how often he asked people to pray for him, even giving specifics on what to pray. Paul placed a high value on others praying for him and his ministry. Let's remind people that we love to pray for them—no matter how often.

And to those of you who hesitate to share your prayer requests, consider what blessings you may be missing.

Lynnette Goebel

Father, how we thank You for the gift of prayer. Give us wisdom to know how to pray, when to ask for prayer, and when to pray for others. Make us mindful of others who need us to pray for them. Keep us mindful, praying in all things. Amen.

The saying is trustworthy, for: If we have died with him, we will also live with him; if we endure, we will also reign with him; if we deny him, he also will deny us; if we are faithless, he remains faithful — for he cannot deny himself.

2 Timothy 2:11-13

*I*t was a case of woman vs. shrub. I had three Rose of Sharon bushes ready to replace the three spiraeas left in my front flower bed. I started by borrowing one of my husband's shovels. Then I plunged the shovel around the bush over and over, trying to force the bush up from its roots. After about a half-hour of this, I wasn't making much progress with the dry, clay-filled soil, but I wasn't giving up!

I pressed harder and harder on the shovel handle until I heard a sharp crack! The shovel handle cracked completely off the spade. Now what?! "We have more shovels. I'll just get another one," I thought. After working at the bush again, soon I heard another sickening crack as the second shovel handle split in two. Seconds later as I lay on my back in the grass, exhausted and ready to quit, my husband drove in.

This wasn't good; I knew these two were his favorite shovels. As I sheepishly confessed right away, I was relieved at his gracious response. He gently said with a smile, "You know, you could have just said 'Honey, could you help me?'"

Ouch! Why is it that it's so easy for me to confuse faithfulness with stubbornness? This case of woman vs. shrub taught me that I can only be faithful by God's strength and His Spirit's direction.

I need His help and the help of others. Being faithful doesn't mean digging in my heels when God is saying it's time to move on.

Also, sometimes I need to wait until the ground is soft before I start digging. By the time I got around to digging up the other two bushes, rain had come. Those bushes came out fairly easily because the ground was soft. I need to seek God concerning the timing of when to start doing His work with people around me. Are their hearts ready?

Finally, the most important lesson I learned from that shrub is that no matter how hard I try, I will get faithfulness wrong in some way or another. I need to remember the One Who is faithful even when I am not.

And...maybe I should add a new shovel to my husband's Christmas list this year.

Wendy McCready

God, I confess that what I like to call faithfulness is often just my being stubborn. Help me to be willing to ask for help when I need it and to follow your Spirit's direction at all times. Amen.

*And the Lord's servant must not be quarrelsome but kind to every-
one, able to teach, patiently enduring evil, correcting his opponents
with gentleness. God may perhaps grant them repentance leading to
a knowledge of the truth.*

2 Timothy 2:24-26

*M*y husband and I have been hurt and blindsided by people
as we minister, and at times, those people don't apologize or
work with us towards reconciliation. We often ask, "How do
we faithfully serve people who have hurt us and continue to
hurt us?" It is so easy to get sucked into a foolish or petty conflict. It's as if someone is poking you with a stick, trying to
goad you into picking up a stick to fight back. In 2 Timothy 2,
Paul is telling us not to pick up the stick. How often do we let
ourselves get drawn into a foolish conflict and treat others
wrongly?

According to Paul, being faithful in ministry means we must
"be kind to everyone." *Everyone* — even the people who poke
at us (or even hit us) with sticks.

We are to "patiently endure evil." There are times when what
we are going through in ministry is evil, plain and simple, yet
we are to endure it patiently.

We are called to "be able to teach." Sometimes, people don't
even know that what they're doing is wrong, and it's our job
to teach them in those situations.

We are to "correct [our] opponents with gentleness." It's often
easy to correct people but to forget the gentleness part. We
need to be like Christ — extending grace and kindness even
though it isn't deserved.

Possibly the hardest part of this passage for me is the last sentence. The only promise here is that **perhaps** God may lead them to repentance, and they **may** come to their senses. It feels a bit unfair that there is no guarantee that the person hurting me will ever change. But that highlights the misdirection of my heart—it's not up to me to change people. It is **God** who may lead them to repentance, not me. My job is to be faithful to Him and to leave the rest in His hands.

We should be faithful to treat people this way because it is an overflow of God's love flowing from us to others. Who is tempting you to pick up the stick today? Which characteristic of the Lord's servant do you struggle with the most? Ask God to help you today.

Tobi Henschel

Lord, please help me to be Your faithful servant. Give me Your kindness, gentleness, and patience towards _____in my ministry. Amen.

The Road of Righteousness *84*

He who dwells in the shelter of the Most High will abide in the shadow of the Almighty. I will say to the LORD, "My refuge and my fortress, my God, in whom I trust.

Psalm 91:1-2

*W*henever I travel anywhere, I enjoy the trip as much as the destination. When driving, my husband and I will often take the backroads just because the view is better and the opportunity for unexpected and, usually pleasant, surprises is so much greater.

I wish I could view my own journey through life with as much excitement as I view a family road trip. As I ponder my own journey toward righteousness, I realize that being righteous is a journey, not an achievement. I need the reminder that God gives us in Psalm 91:1-2. God is my refuge. He is my fortress. Why am I afraid? Often, it's because I have forgotten to follow the path He has set before me, and I have started off on my own journey to nowhere.

Only God can make me righteous, but I need to choose to follow the right paths, to make the right decisions to lead a righteous life. I am at a point in my life where I now recognize that many of the choices that I have made in my recent past were not on God's chosen path for my life. In fact, I'm pretty sure I got right off the road which He set me upon, and I went down a side road to nowhere. It was literally a dead end.

You see, I discovered that just because something was going well did not mean that it was God's will for me. I wasn't growing, I wasn't bearing fruit. I felt like nothing more than a fraud walking into church each Sunday.

Of course, I loved the Lord, but something was missing. I was so caught up in pursuing my own goals for my life that I could not see that I had nothing left to give to anything or anyone else. And God let me go on down my own road, getting further and further away from His will, until, over a short period of time, it all ended, and I deeply regretted everything I had lost by following my own desires.

I have discovered that I can only have one purpose for my journey, and that needs to be the pursuit of righteousness. When I pursue God, when I focus on being like Him, my journey becomes joyful again.

Marcy Ardis

Dear Lord, I trust You and I want to pursue Your plans for my life. I want to live a life that is righteous and wholly given over to Your will for me. Help me to focus only on You and Your will for me rather than on my own desires. Amen.

So we do not lose heart. Though our outer self is wasting away, our inner self is being renewed day by day.

                                                        2 Corinthians 4:16

I would not choose *any* times of grief my husband and I have experienced over 18 years of ministry. But my grief vision is flawed and retrospective. God foresees and oversees each moment of grief in a way that my heart is learning to welcome.

Merriam-Webster Dictionary defines grief as a "deep sadness especially for the loss of someone or something loved." A pastoral couple's call to love the sheep opens a great capacity to be hurt, leading to grief, which opens a great capacity to be healed by the Shepherd.

So how should we grieve?

1. **With truth**. I shed many tears during our first year of marriage, feeling inadequate at the thought of being a pastor's wife. My kind-hearted husband would invite me to sit on his lap, let me cry, and listen as I asked, "Why did you want to marry me, knowing you were called to be a pastor?" My husband would whisper, "Because I love you for exactly who God made you to be — with your own set of gifts." Grieving hearts need to hear truth spoken by those they can trust.

2. **With hope**. Perhaps we never grieve so deeply as when we feel a situation will never change. C.S. Lewis describes grief in *A Grief Observed*: "Her absence is like the sky, spread over everything. "

An absence or loss can cloud our thoughts and feel like the only thing we think about, and for a time that might be reality. When hope does break through our clouds of grief, we might not recognize it, welcome it, or trust it will hold—but with God's faithfulness, hope always holds.

3. **With healing**. "Good Grief" is a booklet written by the late Granger E. Westberg. ABC News Senior Medical Contributor, Dr. Timothy Johnson, MD, says, "This gem is written with the heart of a pastor, the insight of a psychologist, the humanity of a father and husband, and the hope of someone who has seen so many survive the process of grieving." It's vital for pastoral couples to study out the grieving process, not only for personal healing, but also to help point others to healing.

God has been faithful through our share of grief. Let's be known for recounting how God brought us through times of grief with truth, hope, and healing.

Denna Busenitz

Lord God, we ask You to bind up our broken hearts and heal our wounds. Help us not to lose heart, though our outer nature is wasting away; renew our inner nature with Your healing power—day by day. Amen.

Death and life are in the power of the tongue, and those who love it will eat its fruits.

Proverbs 18:21

*Y*ou've probably heard the popular saying, "With great power comes great responsibility." I think this phrase is true of what happens to us when we become pastors' wives. We are regular women who have our own individual struggles and who are thrust into a position of power simply by marrying a man who happens to be a pastor. It's not the power of church politics or influencing decisions — it's the power of our words.

The more important a person is in our lives, the more potent her words are. Think of a coach's words to her athletes, or a teacher's words to his students. A positive word can push that athlete or student to greater heights and accomplishments, while a negative word can stifle him for years to come.

As pastors' wives, our words can be very important to the women of the church. What kind of words will we speak — life words or death words? I am not always good at being careful about what I say, and I have to ask God to set a guard over my mouth (Psalm 141:3)! In reality, all of God's children are called to careful speech. But as a pastor's wife, I want to use my "power," or my influence, for life words. How can I do that?

Don't be salty; be seasoned with salt (Colossians 4:6) – It's so easy to be grumpy and complain! However, I need to have a seasoned response that is full of grace, not complaint.

Don't tear down; build up (Ephesians 4:29) – I need to be purposeful about using words that will encourage and build up others, not criticize or tear down.

Don't be quick to speak; be quick to hear (James 1:19) – I need to remember to slow down and really hear other people. I can show them love by taking the time to hear what they have to say and not just talking at them.

Don't stoke the fire; put out the fire (Proverbs 26:20) – I need to do everything in my power to not stoke the fire of gossip. When someone tells me something she shouldn't, I need to be where it stops, gently reminding her that we shouldn't be talking about it.

How can you build someone up today with your words?

Tobi Henschel

Lord, please set a guard over my mouth! Keep me far away from death words. Fill me with life words that I might build up and encourage others. Amen.

Contribute to the needs of the saints and seek to show hospitality.
                                                    Romans 12:13

When my husband was hired to be the pastor of our church seventeen years ago, God planted an idea which would profoundly characterize our ministry: to have everyone in our congregation to our home for dinner within the first year. We didn't have kids yet, so it was doable.

This kind of hospitality ministry is one of the potential benefits of pastoring a small church in a rural community — you can know everyone in your church. We wanted to get to know everyone, and, living in a town of 1200 people, it was a great way to begin to get plugged in, so we began.

Once or twice a week, we had people over to the parsonage for a home-cooked meal — sometimes delicious, sometimes mediocre. But always, there was a connection. Whether it was a couple, a single mom, a group of widows, or a family, we heard their stories and got to know them — how they came to Christ and their perspectives on the long history of our church.

We laughed and listened to my husband share his raucous stories of growing up in rural Pennsylvania. Often at the end of the evening we heard, "You guys are so down-to-earth!"

That vision God gave us yielded tremendous fruit! We were able to have almost every regular church attender over the first year. By the end of the second year, as we continued this practice with newcomers and further developed relationships, we were well integrated into the church and community.

Hospitality can also be an effective evangelistic tool. When we have non-believers in our home, God provides opportunities to share our testimonies. When we share a meal, we share life. That is what Jesus did—eating with tax-collectors and sinners, affecting influence and change, and building relationships around the table.

How do we do this with busy ministry lives? It doesn't have to be a three-course meal. Invite a family over for hot dogs after church or for pizza on a Friday night. Make s'mores together in the backyard or have a longer dinner together. It doesn't really matter how we do it; it just matters that we take the time to invest, to serve, to show hospitality for the sake of the Gospel.

Jennifer McConnell

Merciful Father, thank you for the connections that are made through the sharing of a meal and for the example Jesus set for us in this work. Use our hands, families, tables, and food for Your glory and for Your Kingdom. Amen.

Getting Down to the Nitty Gritty 88

Therefore, my brothers, whom I love and long for, my joy and crown, stand firm thus in the Lord, my beloved.

Philippians 4:1

*T*rue Grit.

How would you describe the word *grit*?

- small, loose particles of stone or sand
- courage and resolve; strength of character
- clenching (the teeth), especially to keep one's resolve when faced with an unpleasant or painful duty

I recently read a newsletter written by a pastor's wife about the everyday things happening in their small, rural community. As I read, the word *grit* came to mind. Amid celebrations for birthdays, anniversaries, and graduations, the family endured grit (small, loose particles of stone or sand—the kind that irritate and annoy). These things can be illness, drama, gossip, worries, or difficult attacks on the ministry of the church.

As she shared about living and raising a family in a culture completely different from how she was raised, I saw her grit (courage and resolve; strength of character).
The joy and accomplishments of her children in hobbies and activities strange to many of us who don't live in rural settings permeated her news. It takes courage to embrace the unknown. It takes strength of character to thrive in the unfamiliar.

I'm sure she encounters many times when she grits her teeth to keep her resolve when faced with gossip or drama, or loneliness in being far from family...or fiery darts sent from the enemy. And yet, it all comes back to her courage and strength of character, because she is grounded in the Word of God and knows that "all things are possible with God" (Mark 10:27).

The life of a pastor's wife includes struggles and sorrows of which many may not be aware. She often carries the burdens of the church alongside her husband. She may bear the marks of vicious gossip or inconsiderate comments. She may not have the option to turn away from an unpleasant or painful duty.

You are not alone, dear one. Read through Hebrews 11 to see a cloud of witnesses who testify to us of their grit, their faith in Jesus, the Author and Perfecter of our faith.

Lynnette Goebel

Heavenly Father, we pray for pastors' wives around the globe today, asking You to strengthen and encourage them. Thank You for giving them strength of character based on Your Word as they minister in Your church and their communities. Amen.

And we all, with unveiled face, beholding the glory of the Lord, are being transformed into the same image from one degree of glory to another. For this comes from the Lord who is the Spirit.

2 Corinthians 3:18

Social media is full of promises to help you "be your best self" and "live your best life." The premise is that if you have the right job, diet hard enough, work out hard enough, and meditate long enough, you will transform your body and mind into something better than it was before you began your chosen course of action.

All of this sounds good on the surface. Who wouldn't want to transform herself this way? Don't we all want to be the best we can be?

The thing is, our lives are not ours to transform. When we start to believe that we can rely on our own selves to improve what we consider to be our imperfections, we take away our reliance on God's transformational power in our lives. Yes, we can and should make choices that impact our lives in a positive way, but the purpose of doing that is so we can live the life that God has chosen for us.

First Corinthians 6:19 tells us that our bodies are temples of the Holy Spirit and that *"You are not your own"* (*emphasis mine*). Second Corinthians 3:18 further reminds us that we are being transformed into God's image. We need a spiritual transformation to live the life that God has chosen for us. All the physical and mental transforming we attempt to accomplish on our own is useless if we do not allow God to also transform us spiritually to be more and more like Him.

Our lives are not our own. God has plans for each of us that are so much greater than anything we could imagine and work out for ourselves. It's not wrong to want to improve ourselves, and we certainly play a role in making healthy choices in our lives, but we can never be truly changed without acknowledging and relying on God's transformational power in our lives.

Another trip to the gym, another self-help book, another inspirational quote—none of these have the transformational power of relying on God and trusting Him to make us into the person that He wants us to be. We don't need to be our best selves; we need to be the women that God has called us to be.

Marcy Ardis

Dear Lord, transform me according to Your will. I want to be more like You, and I cannot do it on my own. Mould me into the person You want me to become. Amen.

And let us not grow weary of doing good, for in due season we will reap, if we do not give up.

Galatians 6:9

I see a runner nearly every morning on my drive to work. By looking at him, I am guessing that he is about ten or fifteen years older than I am, but he runs rain or shine, snow or sleet, wind or calm. That kind of perseverance and faithfulness inspires me when I think about life in ministry.

As shepherds we are often in the role of regularly calling people out of their sin and into the gospel of grace, and we are called to do it with a spirit of gentleness and with a sobering look at our own tendency to fall into temptation. It can be easy to feel we know more than the people in our congregation because of our level of education or experience with people, but if we forget that we, too, are saved by grace, then we will be deceiving ourselves and fall into trouble.

Each one of us will be held accountable for our own actions and attitudes (Galatians 6:5-7). If we sow kindness, truth, and grace, we will reap the rewards of grace and forgiveness and peace. If we sow bitterness and complaining and envy and selfishness, we will reap strife, unrest, anger, and pain.

Not only do we need to tend to our own heart, but we need to tend to the hearts of others. The call is clear that we are to reach out and restore those who are sinning to bring them to Christ. We ought not to be weary or exhausted or weak as we do good for others because "in due time" we will reap a harvest. How? If we do not give up.

We can only do that by the grace of God, but His grace is enough, and…the promise is great: in just the right time and season we will reap.

As pastors' wives we have the privilege of regularly serving those who belong to the house of God, and by His grace we can do it without losing heart. Like my runner "friend," I want to tirelessly work so that I can reap the rewards of our labor. I don't want to give up either!

Wendy McCready

Lord, it is really hard to keep going some days in ministry. Give me the grace to keep plodding on, knowing that if I don't give up, I will one day see the reward. Amen.

Prayer

May eternity tell the story of the results of our effectual prayers

(from James 5:16b)

*I*n this appendix we offer Scripture prayer guides you can pray for your husband and children. Some are written with blanks so you can insert the names of your loved ones while others are written more as a general guide. Prayer combined with Scripture are powerful weapons against the Enemy, and we want to wield them well.

Encouragement on prayer from a fellow pastor's wife:

"Mismanaged hurt takes ministry people out. We have to forgive. My life-long prayer has been: *'Please give me a tough hide and a tender heart, Lord.'* We all have insecurities, and hurt happens. The enemy wants to target our weak areas, and he loves to sow discord.

"As much as possible, I have asked the Holy Spirit to help me be unoffendable. Rather than gathering offenses and spreading the disease to others, I'm determining to forgive quickly and refuse to read rejection into things that may have nothing to do with me."

> *Joanna Weaver, more than 40 years as a pastor's wife, best-selling author; check out her website:*
> *joannaweaverbooks.com*

Sunday Prayer:
Praying over your Husband-Pastor before the Sermon

*G*od Most High,

Let Your name be exalted on earth as it is lifted up in heaven. Exalt Your name in the hearts of our people; extend Your kingdom in our world — our sphere of influence (Matthew 6:9-10). As my husband prepares to preach Your Word this morning, let Your Spirit go before him into the hearts of his hearers (Exodus 23:20; Psalm 85:13). Prepare their hearts like good, fertile soil to receive Your Word (Luke 8:15). Only *You*, Lord, can do the deep heart transformations.

Let Your Word go forth from my husband's mouth and bring life, set people free, and water the seeds already planted (1 Corinthians 3:6). I pray that the gospel would speed ahead and be honored (2 Thessalonians 3:1). Let the knowledge of You go out in joy and be led forth in peace. Let the hearts of Your people burst into praise before You (Isaiah 55:12).

Revive our worship today as we sing as a congregation. May we ascribe to You the glory due Your name. May we worship You in the splendor of Your holiness (Psalm 29:2). May our people catch a vision of You, high and exalted, seated on Your throne (Isaiah 6:1). Let our worship this morning be filled with awe and wonder.

If we could see You for who You really are, our hearts would be thrilled (2 Chronicles 18:18). I pray against a spirit of boredom or apathy. I pray for renewed vigor in worship. I pray for repentance and confession of sin. I pray for the fullness of the Holy Spirit in each heart that knows you (Luke 11:13; Ephesians 3:19).

If there are unbelievers in attendance today, I pray that the Holy Spirit would be stirring in their hearts — stirring conviction but also drawing them to Yourself. It's Your kindness, Lord, that leads us to repentance (Romans 2:4). I pray that they will bow the knee to King Jesus and exclaim, "God is really among you!" (1 Corinthians 14:24-25). "My heart's desire and prayer for them is that they may be saved" (Romans 10:1). There's no power in human charisma or personality that can save people, but it is only by the power of the Holy Spirit working in their hearts (1 Corinthians 2:4-5).

I pray that every time my husband opens his mouth, words may be given to him to proclaim the mystery of the gospel with boldness (Ephesians 6:18-19). Grant him the ability to speak Your Word with all boldness (Acts 4:29) for Your name's sake. Give him wisdom to apply Your Word to necessary and urgent situations (James 1:5). Give him wisdom beyond his age and experience to be able to counsel those who come to him in need (James 3:17).

I pray that after Your Word is preached that it would bear good fruit (Ezekiel 17:8) and produce a hundred-fold crop (Matthew 13:8). I pray that our people would not merely be hearers of the Word only but would go forth and be doers (James 1:22). Let them not be deceived in thinking that if they just come to church that it is enough! There are a lot of people who are charmed by the Bible, but not enough people who are changed by it. I pray that everyone listening to the Word preached today would internalize what is being said and walk away changed. I pray that they would go out from this place on a mission. Do whatever it takes, Lord, to get the *most* glory from our lives.

In Jesus' name, Amen!

Chelsea Hall

A Prayer for My Pastor's Wife

*T*hank you, Father, for my pastor's wife.

She is one of the happiest people I know. Whenever she sees me, her face brightens into a smile, showing me that she's genuinely glad to see me. Her smile makes me smile back, even if I'm having a fragile day. Her smile warms my heart.

Father, please let my smile do the same for her. Let her know how much I appreciate her.

Thank You for her creativity — from refurbishing furniture to knitting (or is it crocheting?) to crafting — and that she uses her talents to encourage others. Thank You for her compassion. Thank You that I can learn from her example even though she is the same age as my daughter!

Father, show me how I can encourage her, and let me be a godly example to her.

I know the family has many adventures ahead of them this year. Please give wisdom as they plan life as a family of five. Give discernment as they set priorities. Protect time spent with You each day, Lord. Help her develop a strong prayer life. Open her eyes to new truths in Your Word. Comfort her each day, and give her strength to take on the challenges of being a pastor's wife, a mom, and a woman of grace. Give her joy.

Father, open my eyes to how I can lift her up before the throne of grace and help her fight the fiery darts of the enemy.

For pastors' wives all over the globe, Father, raise up women who will pray for them, encourage them, and appreciate them. I ask as well for protection for them from the attacks of the enemy. Protect them in the midst of struggles and challenges. Give them shouts of joy all through the year as they see Your hand leading them. Open their eyes as they read Your Word. Let them grow in love and obedience to You.

May we all realize that we are here at Your pleasure. Help us to do the things that are worth more than anything this world can give us. May we glorify You in our lives this year.

Amen.

Lynnette Goebel

A Prayer for My Pastor's Kids

*H*eavenly Father, thank You for my pastor's family. Thank You for blessing them with three unique children.

Thank You for allowing us the privilege of watching these children grow and for giving us opportunities to pour into their lives through AWANA and Sunday School—or just smiling as we pass in the hallways.

I know it isn't easy to be a pastor's kid. I'm sure there are perks—like always being there for the donuts before Sunday School. But it must be frustrating being asked for the tenth time how they are today. Give them patience and help them to develop an ease with older folks. Help them to realize that they can minister to older people by being patient and kind.

Protect them, Father. Perhaps they have classmates who make fun of them for being the preacher's kids. Perhaps they feel the sting of failure when others think that they should always be doing everything right because they're the preacher's kids. Give them good friends who also love You—friends who encourage them and don't treat them differently because they are the preacher's kids.

Give them a strong testimony—a courageous witness to their classmates, teammates, and teachers. Give them wisdom to know when to confide in their parents.
Help them to embrace the teachings of Your Word. Give them a love for You. Give them a hunger and thirst to follow You completely. Keep them from thinking that they are a Christian because of what their dad does. Keep them from relying on their parents' faith—help them to each develop their own personal faith in You. Give them joy.

Protect them from evil. Keep them strong. Even when they see others doing wrong, give them compassionate hearts with a strong faith.

Help those of us in the church not to expect something more from them just because they are the preacher's kids. Help us to be kind and patient and helpful. Remind us to pray for them. Let them know we love them because You love them, not because they are the preacher's kids. Keep us from ever using them to get to their parents.

Remind them every day of Your love and care for them. And nudge me, Lord, when I can be a blessing to them and to their whole family.

Amen.

Lynnette Goebel

Wife for Life:
Daily Prayers for Pastor-Husbands

I was inspired to put this list of Scripture-prayers together after hearing Di Mathis share her "Wife for Life" list that she prays daily over her husband. Di is a former pastor's wife now serving in pastor-wife care; her husband, Scott, is president of the Fellowship of Berean Churches. Praying for my pastor-husband is one of the most powerful and hard-fought uses of my time. Be encouraged as you pray for your husband!

Denna Busenitz (*with Di Mathis*)

NOTE: The following Scriptures are from the New Living Translation.

MONDAY

Genesis 2:18 *Then the Lord God said, "It is not good for the man to be alone. I will make a helper who is just right for him."*

Lord God, make me a helper just right for my husband, _____, reminding us both that it's not good to be alone. May we together remember that You called the creation of man and woman "very good."

Proverbs 31:10-12 *Who can find a virtuous and capable wife? She is more precious than rubies. Her husband can trust her, and she will greatly enrich his life. She brings him good, not harm, all the days of her life.*

Lord God, help me to greatly enrich my husband's life, allowing me to bring him good and not harm all the days of my life. Make me a virtuous and capable wife who knows her worth is found in Christ. Next to You, let my husband consider me his most precious treasure.

TUESDAY

1 Corinthians 7:1-5 *Now regarding the questions you asked in your letter. Yes, it is good to abstain from sexual relations. But because there is so much sexual immorality, each man should have his own wife, and each woman should have her own husband. The husband should fulfill his wife's sexual needs, and the wife should fulfill her husband's needs. The wife gives authority over her body to her husband, and the husband gives authority over his body to his wife. Do not deprive each other of sexual relations, unless you both agree to refrain from sexual intimacy for a limited time so you can give yourselves more completely to prayer. Afterward, you should come together again so that Satan won't be able to tempt you because of your lack of self-control.*

Lord God, I ask You to bless my husband's and my sex-life, keeping us from any and all sexual immorality. May we together realize, fulfill, and enjoy each other's sexual desires and needs. If we do agree to refrain for a time, let it be so that we can devote ourselves more completely to prayer. In Jesus' powerful name, I ask that Satan would not tempt my husband or me because of lack of self-control, and that we would always come back together.

WEDNESDAY

Ephesians 5:33 *So again I say, each man must love his wife as he loves himself, and the wife must respect her husband.*

Colossians 3:18 *Wives, submit to your husbands, as is fitting for those who belong to the Lord.*

Lord God, enable my husband, _____, to love me as he loves himself; help me to see and appreciate the ways he seeks to do this. Lord God, enable me to respect my husband; help him to see and appreciate it when I do. Let us together rejoice in how fitting these actions are for those who belong to You!

1 Peter 3:1-6 *In the same way, you wives must accept the authority of your husbands. Then, even if some refuse to obey the Good News, your godly lives will speak to them without any words. They will be won over by observing your pure and reverent lives. Don't be concerned about the outward beauty of fancy hairstyles, expensive jewelry, or beautiful clothes. You should clothe yourselves instead with the beauty that comes from within, the unfading beauty of a gentle and quiet spirit, which is so precious to God. This is how the holy women of old made themselves beautiful. They put their trust in God and accepted the authority of their husbands. For instance, Sarah obeyed her husband, Abraham, and called him her master. You are her daughters when you do what is right without fear of what your husbands might do.*

Lord God, help me to live and model a godly life of purity and holy reverence as I also accept the authority of my husband, _____, in my life. Let me be free of outward bondage to beauty and instead clothe myself with an inner beauty that comes from spending time with You. I trust You, God; help me to trust Your workings in my husband, _____, too. May I be as Sarah was to Abraham, not letting fear be my master.

THURSDAY

Colossians 1:9-14 *So we have not stopped praying for you since we first heard about you. We ask God to give you complete knowledge of his will and to give you spiritual wisdom and understanding. Then the way you live will always honor and please the Lord, and your lives will produce every kind of good fruit. All the while, you will grow as you learn to know God better and better. We also pray that you will be strengthened with all his glorious power so you will have all the endurance and patience you need. May you be filled with joy, always thanking the Father. He has enabled you to share in the inheritance that belongs to his people, who live in the light. For he has rescued us from the kingdom of darkness and transferred us into the Kingdom of his dear Son, who purchased our freedom and forgave our sins.*

Lord God, I pray that You would give my husband, _____, complete knowledge of Your will along with all spiritual wisdom and understanding into every aspect of life and ministry today. Whether he's studying, shepherding, working, disciplining, evangelizing, counseling, visiting, resting/rejuvenating, or spending time with family, I pray that he will live in a way that honors and pleases You. May his life produce every kind of good fruit as he grows closer to You.

I pray that You would strengthen my husband, _____, with all Your glorious power so that he will have the endurance and patience he needs. May You fill him with joy and thanksgiving. Thank You for rescuing him from darkness and allowing him to serve You; remind him that You purchased his freedom. Help him to walk in Your forgiveness from sins.

FRIDAY

Romans 12:11 *Never be lazy, but work hard and serve the Lord enthusiastically.*

Lord God, may my husband, _____, never be lazy but work hard and serve You with enthusiasm.

Psalm 115:14 *May the Lord richly bless both you and your children.*

Lord God, may You richly bless my husband, _____, our marriage, and the lives of our children.

SATURDAY

Titus 2:1-8 *As for you, Titus, promote the kind of living that reflects wholesome teaching. Teach the older men to exercise self-control, to be worthy of respect, and to live wisely. They must have sound faith and be filled with love and patience. Similarly, teach the older women to live in a way that honors God. They must not slander others or be heavy drinkers. Instead, they should teach others what is good. These older women must train the younger women to love their husbands and their children, to live wisely and be pure, to work in their homes, to do good, and to be submissive to their husbands. Then they will not bring shame on the word of God. In the same way, encourage the young men to live wisely. And you yourself must be an example to them by doing good works of every kind. Let everything you do reflect the integrity and seriousness of your teaching. Teach the truth so that your teaching can't be criticized. Then those who oppose us will be ashamed and have nothing bad to say about us.*

Lord God, may my husband, _____, promote the kind of living that reflects wholesome teaching. May he teach other men to exercise self-control, be worthy of respect, and live wisely even as You teach him how. May my husband have sound faith and be filled with love and patience. May I teach other women to live in a way that honors God even as You teach me how. May I not slander others or be a heavy drinker, instead teaching others what is good.

May I train younger women to love their husbands and children, showing them how to live wisely. Together and with Your help, may my husband and I encourage others to live wisely as we teach the truth, knowing that when we face opposition, we don't need to be ashamed and fear that others will say bad things about us. May we stand firm in the truth of God's Word together.

SUNDAY

Colossians 1:25-28 *God has given me the responsibility of serving his church by proclaiming his entire message to you. This message was kept secret for centuries and generations past, but now it has been revealed to God's people. For God wanted them to know that the riches and glory of Christ are for you Gentiles, too. And this is the secret: Christ lives in you. This gives you assurance of sharing his glory. So we tell others about Christ, warning everyone and teaching everyone with all the wisdom God has given us. We want to present them to God, perfect in their relationship to Christ.*

Lord God, I thank You that my husband, _____, like the apostle Paul, has been given the responsibility of serving Your church by proclaiming the Gospel message in its entirety, remembering that You live in him! I pray that my husband would proclaim Christ clearly, warn boldly, and teach faithfully those to whom he ministers so they may become mature in Christ.

2 Timothy 1:7 *For God has not given us a spirit of fear and timidity, but of power, love, and self-discipline.*

Lord God, I pray that You will infuse my husband, _____, with courage, calmness, clarity, and passion while he speaks from the pulpit and with the people whom he shepherds. May he not have a spirit of fear, but of power, love, and a sound mind.

Mom for Life:
Daily Prayers for Pastors' Kids

I see parallels to a pastor's family in the movie *The Incredibles 2*. Mr. and Mrs. Incredible and their children, Violet, Dash, and Jack-Jack, seek to walk a threefold, impossible family balance: use superpowers to help save the day for others, live undercover to abide by the new law that makes superheroes illegal, and *also* protect their kids from harm. Violet's words move me — "I renounce superpowers!" — as she shoves her superhero costume into the dish drain and turns on the power-shredding garbage-disposal button, hoping to be rid of what identifies her as a superhero's kid. Are pastors' kids ever tempted to *renounce* their identity as pastors' kids? Ask them sometime; pray for them daily.

Denna Busenitz

NOTE: The following Scriptures are from the New Living Translation.

MONDAY

2 Thessalonians 1:11-12 *So we keep on praying for you, asking our God to enable you to live a life worthy of his call. May he give you the power to accomplish all the good things your faith prompts you to do. Then the name of our Lord Jesus will be honored because of the way you live, and you will be honored along with him. This is all made possible because of the grace of our God and Lord, Jesus Christ.*

Proverbs 2:1-4 *My child, listen to what I say, and treasure my commands. Tune your ears to wisdom, and concentrate on understanding. Cry out for insight, and ask for understanding. Search for them as you would for silver; seek them like hidden treasures.*

Lord God, I keep praying that _____ would live a life worthy of Your call. Give _____ the power to accomplish all the good things his/her faith prompts him/her to do. May _____ honor the name of the Lord Jesus by how he/she lives, made possible by Your grace. I pray that _____ would listen to the wise counsel found in God's Word, treasuring God's commands. May _____ tune his/her ears to wisdom, concentrate on understanding, cry out for insight, and ask for understanding today as he/she starts another week.

TUESDAY

Psalm 28:7 *The Lord is my strength and shield. I trust him with all my heart. He helps me, and my heart is filled with joy. I burst out in songs of thanksgiving.*

Proverbs 4:23-25 *Guard your heart above all else, for it determines the course of your life. Avoid all perverse talk; stay away from corrupt speech. Look straight ahead, and fix your eyes on what lies before you.*

Hebrews 12:2a *We do this by keeping our eyes on Jesus, the champion who initiates and perfects our faith.*

Proverbs 3:5-8 *Trust in the Lord with all your heart; do not depend on your own understanding. Seek his will in all you do, and he will show you which path to take. Don't be impressed with your own wisdom. Instead, fear the Lord and turn away from evil. Then you will have healing for your body and strength for your bones.*

Lord God, I ask You to be _____'s strength and shield as he/she trusts in You. May his/her heart be filled with joy and burst out in songs of thanksgiving. Guard _____'s heart above all else, thus determining the course of his/her life. Protect _____ from the world's influence and help him/her to avoid perverse talk and to stay away from corrupt speech; may the springs of life flow forth in and through him/her. May _____ fix his/her gaze on what lies before him/her, keeping his/her eyes on Jesus who perfects his/her faith. I pray that_____ would not depend on his/her own understanding but rather seek Your will in all. May _____ fear the Lord and turn from evil. I pray that You would heal _____'s body physically, emotionally, and spiritually.

WEDNESDAY

Daniel 1

Psalm 1:1-3 *Oh, the joys of those who do not follow the advice of the wicked, or stand around with sinners, or join in with mockers. But they delight in the law of the Lord, meditating on it day and night. They are like trees planted along the riverbank, bearing fruit each season. Their leaves never wither, and they prosper in all they do.*

Galatians 5:22-23 *But the Holy Spirit produces this kind of fruit in our lives: love, joy, peace, patience, kindness, goodness, faithfulness, gentleness, and self-control. There is no law against these things!*

Lord God, I pray that _____would have wise and godly friends (as Daniel had Shadrach, Meshach, and Abednego), and that together they would stand firm in Your truth, avoiding the way of the wicked. May_____'s delight be in the law of the Lord, meditating on it day and night. May he/she be like a tree planted along the riverbank of God's Word, bearing spiritual fruit (love, joy, peace, patience, kindness, goodness, faithfulness, gentleness, self-control) in every season, prospering in all he/she does.

THURSDAY

Isaiah 30:19-21 *O people of Zion, who live in Jerusalem, you will weep no more. He will be gracious if you ask for help. He will surely respond to the sound of your cries. Though the Lord gave you adversity for food and suffering for drink, he will still be with you to teach you. You will see your teacher with your own eyes. Your own ears will hear him. Right behind you a voice will say, "This is the way you should go," whether to the right or to the left.*

Psalm 34:13 *Then keep your tongue from speaking evil and your lips from telling lies.*

Psalm 19:14 *May the words of my mouth and the meditation of my heart be pleasing to you, O Lord, my rock and my redeemer.*

Lord God, I pray that You would be gracious to _____ when he/she asks You for help. May he/she weep no more as You respond to his/her cries. Use adversity and suffering to teach _____ that You care deeply and promise to never leave or forsake us. I ask that You keep _____ honest in words and actions. Keep _____'s tongue from evil and his/her lips from speaking lies. I pray that all his/her words would be pleasing to You and edifying to others. May _____'s heart also be pleasing to You, and may he/she declare that You are his/her Rock and Redeemer.

FRIDAY

Galatians 5:25 *Since we are living by the Spirit, let us follow the Spirit's leading in every part of our lives.*

Psalm 121:1-3 *I look up to the mountains — does my help come from there? My help comes from the Lord, who made heaven and earth! He will not let you stumble; the one who watches over you will not slumber.*

Lord God, help _____ to live by and follow the Spirit's every leading. Let _____ not become conceited or proud but realize his/her talents and abilities come from You. May _____ lift his/her eyes to the hills and mountains of Your creation and know his/her help comes solely from You.
Let _____ not stumble, but keep him/her on the path You have mapped out. Watch over _____ even as he/she sleeps, being mindful and thankful that You do not slumber.

SATURDAY

Ecclesiastes 9:10 *Whatever you do, do well. For when you go to the grave, there will be no work or planning or knowledge or wisdom.*

Ecclesiastes 11:6 *Plant your seed in the morning and keep busy all afternoon, for you don't know if profit will come from one activity or another — or maybe both.*

Matthew 6:20-21 *Store your treasures in heaven, where moth and rust cannot destroy, and thieves do not break in and steal. Wherever your treasure is, there the desires of your heart will also be.*

Lord God, I pray that _____ would be diligent in his/her work, doing well in whatever he/she does, realizing the eternal value in storing up treasures in Heaven. May You bless, confirm, and establish everything he/she puts effort into.

SUNDAY

Psalm 122:1 *I was glad when they said to me, "Let us go to the house of the Lord."*

Isaiah 40:29-31 *He gives power to the weak and strength to the powerless. Even youths will become weak and tired, and young men will fall in exhaustion. But those who trust in the Lord will find new strength. They will soar high on wings like eagles. They will run and not grow weary. They will walk and not faint.*

Numbers 6:25-26 *May the Lord smile on you and be gracious to you. May the Lord show you his favor and give you his peace.*

Lord God, may _____ be glad to meet in Your house to worship and fellowship. If he/she gets tired of attending church as a pastor's kid, may he/she rely on Your strength and soar high on wings like eagles, run and not grow weary, walk and not faint. May _____ trust in You to find new strength. I boldly ask that You would keep _____ from long periods of rebellion, that he/she might choose to follow Christ instead of the world. I pray that _____ would love, serve, and follow JESUS all the days of his/her life. May the Lord smile on _____ and be gracious to him/her. May the Lord show _____ His favor and give him/her peace.

Prayers for the Pastor's Family:
Character Traits

Prayers written by Deb Lindstrom

NOTE: The following Scriptures are from the New International Version

ACTIONS

Psalm 25:20-21 *Guard my life and rescue me; do not let me be put to shame, for I take refuge in you. May integrity and uprightness protect me, because my hope, Lord-, is in you.*

Lord, guard _____' s life and rescue him/her. Let _____ not be put to shame. Let him/her take refuge in You. May integrity and righteousness protect _____, because his/her hope is in You.

Ephesians 3:16-19 *I pray that out of his glorious riches he may strengthen you with power through his Spirit in your inner being, so that Christ may dwell in your hearts through faith. And I pray that you, being rooted and established in love, may have power, together with all the Lord's holy people, to grasp how wide and long and high and deep is the love of Christ, and to know this love that surpasses knowledge – that you may be filled to the measure of all the fullness of God.*

Lord, I pray that out of Your glorious riches, _____ may be strengthened with power through Your Spirit in his/her inner being, so that Christ may dwell in his/her heart through faith. And I pray that _____, being rooted and established in love, may have power to grasp how wide and long and high and deep is the love of Christ.

I pray that _____ would know this love that surpasses knowledge, so that he/she may be filled to the measure of all Your fullness.

Ephesians 4:1-3 *As a prisoner for the Lord, then, I urge you to live a life worthy of the calling you have received. Be completely humble and gentle; be patient, bearing with one another in love. Make every effort to keep the unity of the Spirit through the bond of peace.*

Lord, may _____ live a life worthy of the calling he/she has received. May _____ be completely humble, gentle and patient, bearing with others in love. May he/she make every effort to keep the unity of the Spirit through the bond of peace.

Ephesians 5:1-2 *Follow God's example, therefore, as dearly loved children and walk in the way of love, just as Christ loved us and gave himself up for us as a fragrant offering and sacrifice to God.*

Lord, may _____ be an imitator of You and understand that he/she is a dearly loved child. May he/she live a life of love, just as Christ loved him/her and gave Himself up for him/her.

Philippians 1:9-11 *And this is my prayer: that your love may abound more and more in knowledge and depth of insight, so that you may be able to discern what is best and may be pure and blameless for the day of Christ, filled with the fruit of righteousness that comes through Jesus Christ — to the glory and praise of God.*

Lord, I pray that _____'s love may abound still more and more in knowledge and depth of insight (discernment), so that he/she may discern what is best and may be pure and blameless until the day of Christ. May _____ be filled with the fruit of righteousness, which comes through Jesus Christ.

Colossians 1:9-12 *For this reason, since the day we heard about you, we have not stopped praying for you. We continually ask God to fill you with the knowledge of his will through all the wisdom and understanding that the Spirit gives, so that you may live a life worthy of the Lord and please him in every way: bearing fruit in every good work, growing in the knowledge of God, being strengthened with all power according to his glorious might so that you may have great endurance and patience, and giving joyful thanks to the Father, who has qualified you to share in the inheritance of his holy people in the kingdom of light.*

Lord, I pray that You would fill _____ with the knowledge of Your will through all spiritual wisdom and understanding. I pray that he/she would live a life worthy of You and please You in every way.
I pray that _____ will bear fruit in every good work and that he/she would grow in the knowledge of You. Strengthen _____ with all power according to Your glorious might so that he/she will have endurance and patience and joyfully give thanks to You.

ATTITUDE

Ephesians 4:31-33 *Get rid of all bitterness, rage and anger, brawling and slander, along with every form of malice. Be kind and compassionate to one another, forgiving each other, just as in Christ God forgave you.*

Lord Jesus, may _____ get rid of all bitterness, rage and anger, brawling and slander, along with every form of malice. May _____ be kind and compassionate to others, and forgive others as You have forgiven him/her.

Philippians 2:3-5 *Do nothing out of selfish ambition or vain conceit. Rather, in humility value others above yourselves, not looking to your own interests but each of you to the interests of the others. In your relationships with one another, have the same mindset as Christ Jesus.*

Lord, I pray that _____ would have the same attitude as Christ. May he/she do nothing out of selfish ambition or vain conceit. Help _____ to be humble and to see others as better than himself/herself. Help _____ to not just look to his/her own interests, but also to the interests of others.

Colossians 2:6-7 *So then, just as you received Christ Jesus as Lord, continue to live your lives in him, rooted and built up in him, strengthened in the faith as you were taught, and overflowing with thankfulness.*

Lord, I pray that _____ would continue to live in Christ. May he/she be rooted and built up in Him, strengthened in the faith and overflowing with thankfulness.

BATTLE/ENEMY

Ephesians 6:10-17 *Finally, be strong in the Lord and in his mighty power. Put on the full armor of God, so that you can take your stand against the devil's schemes. For our struggle is not against flesh and blood, but against the rulers, against the authorities, against the powers of this dark world and against the spiritual forces of evil in the heavenly realms. Therefore put on the full armor of God, so that when the day of evil comes, you may be able to stand your ground, and after you have done everything, to stand.*
Stand firm then, with the belt of truth buckled around your waist, with the breastplate of righteousness in place, and with your feet fitted with the readiness that comes from the gospel of peace. In addition to all this, take up the shield of faith, with which you can extinguish all the flaming arrows of the evil one. Take the helmet of salvation and the sword of the Spirit, which is the word of God.

Dear Lord, help _____ to be strong in You and Your mighty power. Help him/her to put on Your full armor so that he/she can stand firm against the devil's schemes. May _____ stand firm, wearing the belt of truth, the breastplate of righteousness, feet fitted with the readiness that comes from the gospel of peace, the shield of faith, the helmet of salvation, and the sword of the Spirit.

HEART and MIND

Psalm 73:21-28 *When my heart was grieved and my spirit embittered, I was senseless and ignorant; I was a brute beast before you. Yet I am always with you; you hold me by my right hand. You guide me with your counsel, and afterward you will take me into glory. Whom have I in heaven but you? And earth has nothing I desire besides you. My flesh and my heart may fail, but God is the strength of my heart and my portion forever. Those who are far from you will perish; you destroy all who are unfaithful to you. But as for me, it is good to be near God. I have made the Sovereign Lord my refuge; I will tell of all your deeds.*

Lord, please remind _____ that You are always with him/her and that You hold him/her by his/her right hand. Please guide _____ with Your counsel all of his/her life. May _____ desire You and may his/her heart be strengthened by You. May You be _____'s portion forever, and may Your nearness be essential to him/her. Help _____ to make You his/her refuge and to tell of all Your deeds.

Ephesians 1:17-19a *I keep asking that the God of our Lord Jesus Christ, the glorious Father, may give you the Spirit of wisdom and revelation, so that you may know him better. I pray that the eyes of your heart may be enlightened in order that you may know the hope to which he has called you, the riches of his glorious inheritance in his holy people, and his incomparably great power for us who believe.*

Lord, may You, the God of our Lord Jesus Christ, the glorious Father, give _____ the Spirit of wisdom and revelation (Christ), so that he/she may know Christ better. May the eyes of _____'s heart be enlightened in order that he/she may know the hope to which
You have called him/her, the riches of Your glorious inheritance to the saints, and Your incomparably great power for those who believe.

Philippians 4:6-7 *Do not be anxious about anything, but in every situation, by prayer and petition, with thanksgiving, present your requests to God. And the peace of God, which transcends all understanding, will guard your hearts and your minds in Christ Jesus.*

Lord, I pray that _____ will not be anxious about anything but would pray about everything and be thankful. I pray that, as a result, Your peace that surpasses all understanding would guard _____'s heart in Christ Jesus.

Philippians 4:8 *Finally, brothers and sisters, whatever is true, whatever is noble, whatever is right, whatever is pure, whatever is lovely, whatever is admirable – if anything is excellent or praiseworthy – think about such things.*

Lord, I pray that _____ would think on things that are true, noble, right, pure, lovely, admirable, praiseworthy and excellent.

Colossians 2:1-4 *I want you to know how hard I am contending for you and for those at Laodicea, and for all who have not met me personally. My goal is that they may be encouraged in heart and united in love, so that they may have the full riches of complete understanding, in order that they may know the mystery of God, namely, Christ, in whom are hidden all the treasures of wisdom and knowledge. I tell you this so that no one may deceive you by fine-sounding arguments.*

Lord, I pray that _____ may be encouraged in heart and united in love with the body of Christ, so that he/she may have the full riches of complete understanding and know Christ, in whom are hidden all the treasures of wisdom and knowledge, so that he/she will not be deceived by fine-sounding arguments.

Colossians 3:1-2 *Since, then, you have been raised with Christ, set your hearts on things above, where Christ is, seated at the right hand of God. Set your minds on things above, not on earthly things.*

Lord, I pray that _____ would set his/her heart on things above, where Christ is seated at Your right hand. May _____ set his/her mind on things above, not on earthly things.

For the following section, substitute "Jesus" for any reference to God's Word, Law (statutes, decrees, commands), and wisdom. The Bible says that Jesus is the Word, fulfills the Law, and is the Wisdom of God.

ACTIONS

Psalm 19:12-14 *But who can discern their own errors? Forgive my hidden faults. Keep your servant also from willful sins; may they not rule over me. Then I will be blameless, innocent of great transgression. May these words of my mouth and this meditation of my heart be pleasing in your sight, Lord, my Rock and my Redeemer.*

Lord, reveal any hidden faults in _____. Keep him/her also from willful sins; may they not rule over _____. Then he/she will be blameless, innocent of great transgression. May the words of his/her mouth and the meditation of his/her heart be pleasing in Your sight. May You be _____'s Lord, Rock, and Redeemer

HEART

Psalm 119:9-16 *How can a young person stay on the path of purity? By living according to your word. I seek you with all my heart; do not let me stray from your commands. I have hidden your word in my heart that I might not sin against you. Praise be to you, Lord; teach me your decrees. With my lips I recount all the laws that come from your mouth. I rejoice in following your statutes as one rejoices in great riches. I meditate on your precepts and consider your ways. I delight in your decrees; I will not neglect your word.*

Lord God, help _____ to keep his/her way pure by living according to Your Word (Christ). May _____ seek You with all his/her heart and not stray from Your commands (Jesus). Help him/her to hide Your Word (Jesus) in his/her heart so that he/she will not sin against You.
Teach _____ Your decrees (Jesus) and help him/her to rejoice in following Your statutes (Jesus), to meditate on Your precepts (Jesus), and to consider Your ways. Lord, help _____ not to neglect Your Word (Jesus).

WALK

Proverbs 4:11-13 *I instruct you in the way of wisdom and lead you along straight paths. When you walk, your steps will not be hampered; when you run, you will not stumble. Hold on to instruction, do not let it go; guard it well, for it is your life.*

Lord, may wisdom (Jesus) guide and lead _____ along straight paths. When he/she walks, let his/her steps not be hampered; when he/she runs, let him/her not stumble. May _____ hold on to instruction (Jesus), not let it (Him) go, and guard it (Him) well, for it (He) is his/her life.

YOUR WORD

Psalm 119:33-37 *Teach me, Lord, the way of your decrees, that I may follow it to the end. Give me understanding, so that I may keep your law and obey it with all my heart. Direct me in the path of your commands, for there I find delight. Turn my heart toward your statutes and not toward selfish gain. Turn my eyes away from worthless things; preserve my life according to your word.*

Teach _____, O Lord, to follow Your decrees (Christ), that he/she would keep them to the end. Give _____ understanding so that he/she will keep Your Law (Christ) and obey it (Him) with all his/her heart. Direct _____ in the path of Your commands (Christ) and help him/her to find delight there. Turn his/her heart toward Your statutes (Christ) and away from selfish gain and worthless things. Preserve _____'s life according to Your Word (Jesus).

PASTOR-HUSBAND

Ephesians 6:19-20 *Pray also for me, that whenever I speak, words may be given me so that I will fearlessly make known the mystery of the gospel, for which I am an ambassador in chains. Pray that I may declare it fearlessly, as I should.*

Lord, I pray that whenever _____ opens his mouth, You would give him the words to fearlessly make known the mystery of the gospel. May _____ declare the gospel fearlessly.

Finding Hope Amidst Depression: Praying Psalm 6

A wise friend told my husband, "We can't be doing the ministry in such a way that it ruins God's ministry in and to us. So, changes are needed and sometimes large changes. Our calling is first to Christ, then to our wife, then to our children. Our church can always find another pastor, but our wife has one husband, our kids—one dad, and our walk with Christ cannot be sacrificed."

Those words echoed in my soul as I walked alongside my husband as he battled depression. The desire to not sacrifice my walk with Christ on the altar of fear forced me to slow down, be still, and pray with boldness and confidence. I wanted my husband to persevere in this trial, but that meant I also had to learn to persevere in prayer. To aid me in this endeavor, I prayed through the psalms.

Sections emerged in Psalm 6 as I read. The psalmist begs for mercy. "Do not rebuke me...nor chasten me ...be gracious to me...heal me...return...rescue me...save my soul ." (vv. 1-2, 4). He appeals to God's undeserving love and mercy: "Save me because of your loving kindness" (v. 4b).

The psalmist grieves (vv. 6-7). He expresses great sorrow. Is God correcting him? Is this an attack from the enemy? The psalmist searches his heart before the Lord.

The psalmist declares his confidence in the Lord (vv. 8-10). The psalmist, once dismayed, now declares his enemies will be ashamed and greatly dismayed because the Lord has heard his prayers.
I prayed these sections over my husband, inserting his name and details as appropriate.

(Prayer based on NASB Translation)

Lord, do not rebuke _____ in Your anger, nor chasten him in Your wrath. Be gracious, O Lord, for he is pining away. Heal him, for his soul is greatly dismayed. How long will this last? Return, O Lord! Rescue his soul! Save him because of Your lovingkindness. Let him live so he can praise Your name. He is weary with crying; he is wasting away with grief. His strong adversaries feel impossible to defeat. Make them depart.

Lord, You have heard his weeping. You have heard his pleas, and You receive this prayer. No matter how it looks, I will believe that You will cause his enemies to turn back and be ashamed, even the enemy of depression.

Stacey Weeks

Finding Hope Amidst Depression:
Praying Psalm 86

*P*salm 86 gave words to my grief and fears when I didn't know what or how to pray. It helped me persevere in prayer on behalf of my family when I was emotionally depleted. It helped me to hope in God.

As we read Psalm 86, categories emerge. The psalmist makes declarations about God, thoughts about himself, he resolves to act, and he makes requests. Nearly every word from Psalm 86 lands in one of these categories. I followed the psalmist's pattern and prayed for my husband, beginning with God's character and ending with our need.

(Prayer based on NASB Translation)

Lord, You are good, forgiving, and abundant in lovingkindness. You answer our prayers. There is none like You and no works like Yours. All nations will worship and glorify You because You are great. You are _____'s Deliverer and Comforter. You are merciful, gracious, patient, and true. We revere, obey, and trust You. We cry out to You because we are afflicted and needy. It feels as if our enemies have risen against us, but we call upon You in confidence. We will walk in Your truth, give thanks, and glorify Your name.

I humbly ask that You would incline Your ear and answer _____'s prayer. He's begging to be saved from his enemies. He asks for your grace, for his soul to be glad, and for you to notice his need. Teach him Your ways, unite his heart to fear You, turn him to You, and grant him strength. Show him a sign for good that haters will see and be ashamed.

Stacey Weeks

Benediction Prayer

*P*recious Ever-Present Father, in Your kindness, wisdom, mercy and grace, bring about beautiful flowering growth — growth from the seeds You have already planted in the hearts of my precious sister pastors' wives.

Let these be seeds of sincere, wholehearted love for You first and then for their families and those to whom they minister; seeds of deeply rooted joy that exude pleasure in Your presence through whatever You take them; seeds of the peace that can't be explained even in the darkest valleys; seeds of patience that bears with those they love even when tested beyond human ability; seeds of kindness of heart and goodness of deed that express themselves unselfishly and willingly; seeds of faithfulness, gentleness and self-control that demonstrate they are truly children of their Heavenly Father.

May the flowerbeds of Your work in them grow in beauty and abundance and be ever-increasing evidence of Your glory, adorning the Gospel and Christ in and through them.

Mary Courts

Endnotes

#13

I. Howard Marshall. *1 Peter (The IVP New Testament Commentary Series, Volume 17)*. (Downers Grove, Illinois: IVP Academic, 2011).

#14

Erwin Lutzer *He Will Be the Preacher: The Story of God's Providence in My Life*. (Chicago, Illinois: Moody Publishers, 2015).

#17

Marilyn Damron. *A Practical Guide to the Caring for the Heart Model of Prayer*. Caring for the Heart Ministries, Inc., 2018. Kindle edition.

#36

Elisabeth Elliot. *Let Me Be a Woman: Notes to My Daughter on the Meaning of Womanhood*. (Wheaton, Illinois: Tyndale House, 1976).

#46

Charles Augustus Keeler. *The Simple Home*. (San Francisco, California: Paul Elder and Company Publishers, 1904).

#50

Pete Docter and Ronnie Del Carmen. *Inside Out*. Walt Disney Studios Motion Pictures, 2015.

#51

Lucy Maud Montgomery. *Anne of Green Gables*. (Boston, Massachusetts: L.C. Page & Company Inc., 1908).

#56

G. K. Chesterton. *The Crimes of England*. (New York, New York: John Lane Company, 1916).

John Piper. *A Hunger for God: Desiring God through Fasting and Prayer*. (Wheaton, Illinois: Crossway, 2013).

#59

Paul David Tripp. *What Did You Expect? Redeeming the Realities of Marriage*. (Wheaton, Illinois: Crossway, 2015).

#64

Christine Hoover. "Shona Murray on Fighting an Allegiance to Busyness." By Faith with Christine Hoover, 2020, www.buzzsprout.com/150937/2645875.

#73

Sally Burke and Cyndie Claypool de Neve. *Raise Them Up: Praying God's Word Over Your Kids*. (Eugene, Oregon: Harvest House Publishers, 2019).

#74

Jen Wilkin. *None Like Him: 10 Ways God Is Different from Us (and Why That's a Good Thing)*. (Wheaton, Illinois: Crossway, 2016).

#85

C.S. Lewis. *A Grief Observed*. (London, United Kingdom: Faber & Faber, 1961).

Granger E. Westberg. *Good Grief*. 50th Anniversary Edition. (Minneapolis Minnesota: Fortress Press, 2011).

"Grief." *Miriam Webster*, www.merriam-webster.com/dictionary/grief. Accessed 26 Apr. 2021.

Prayers

Brad Bird. *The Incredibles*. Buena Vista Pictures, 2004.

Contributors

Marcy Ardis
Writer
Marcy and her husband, Gord, live in the country in southwestern Ontario where they serve in two rural, small-town churches. Marcy recently retired from teaching high school in a nearby community and now enjoys having the freedom to homeschool her daughter. When she has free time she likes going for walks with her family, gardening, doing genealogical research, reading local history books, and exploring nearby provincial parks.

Amber Beery
Guest Writer
Amber lives in mid-Michigan with her husband, Matt, and their three children. They serve a small church and desire to learn and grow with the entire body of Christ, including those with disability. Amber has a Bachelor of Arts in print media communications and works as a social media coordinator. Having grown up on a farm in Kansas, Amber is a fan of wide-open spaces and thunderstorms.

Mel Boyle
Board of Reference
Mel is serves with her husband, Mike, who is currently serving as an interim pastor in Illinois. They have planted two churches and also served with the Evangelical Free Church of America (EFCA) in the Dakotas. Mike was a professor of Pastoral Studies at Moody Bible Institute for 11 years. Mel has a Bachelor of Arts in Elementary Education from the University of North Dakota. She enjoys encouraging pastors' wives and being involved in women's ministry and Bible studies. She also enjoys time with her eight grandchildren!

Denna Busenitz
Director/Writer/Speaker
Denna and her husband, Kurt, have five children and have been church planters with Rural Home Missionary Association (RHMA) in the Sandhills Region of Nebraska for almost 20 years. Kurt pastors Sandhills Church of Hope—"one church with two locations" in small-town and rural Nebraska. Denna has a music degree from Moody Bible Institute and helps coordinate music at church. Her weeks are filled with Moms in Prayer groups, kids club/youth ministries, and organizing the family calendar. She serves on her local grocery store board and subs at school.

Sarah Chadbourn
Guest Writer
Sarah and her husband, Jonathan, are from third-generational ministry families. Their ministry experiences began in France as church planters. They then moved to a small Illinois town to help strengthen and experience the God-guided growth of a struggling church. Sarah's husband is the pastor of education at Cornerstone Baptist Church in Groveland, Illinois, where she enjoys the busy life of a pastor's wife. Sarah earned a degree in Nutritional Counseling from Calvary Bible College, where she and Jonathan met. She enjoys writing, counseling, and speaking God's truth to women of all ages. In her free time she enjoys playing piano, jogging, reading out loud to her five children, and decorating her house.

Mary Courts
Board of Reference
Mary and her husband, Sam, have served in rural pastoral ministry with Village Missions since 1998. They ministered in a tiny town in Nebraska for 16 years and are currently serving in Deer Trail, Colorado. She volunteers at an area crisis pregnancy/women's resource center. She has also worked for many years as an Awana Cubbies leader/teacher and as the worship/music planner for their congregation. She loves to

facilitate women's Bible study groups and occasionally speaks for ladies retreats and special events.

Amber Fox
Website Manager/Writer
Amber's passion is to help moms first love Jesus and then teach them to serve Him by ministering to their families. She desires to make a generational difference for an eternal perspective. Together with her husband, Ben, she keeps busy raising seven children to love Jesus and to serve Him. Ben has been a pastor for seventeen years. They are currently in ministry transition, serving in Upper Michigan and Wisconsin. She blogs at cultivatingagodlyhome.com and is the author of *The Homeschooling Housewife: Juggling it ALL, One Priority at a Time.*

Lynnette Goebel
Writer of Flowers for MY Pastor's Wife/Editor
 Lynnette is the Director of Operations at Rural Home Missionary Association (RHMA) Headquarters in Morton, Illinois. She has attended the same small-town church for most of her life. She writes Flowers for MY Pastor's Wife on the Flowers blog because her grandmother, aunt, and sister-in-law were pastors' wives. She adores her pastor's wife, and she wants to encourage all pastors' wives in their ministries.

Chelsea Hall
Writer/Speaker
Chelsea is a pastor's wife in transition. She and her husband, Benji, have been in ministry for almost twelve years together, starting out as youth pastors in 2009. Her husband has just begun a Student Pastor position in Charlottesville, Virginia. They have four children — Silas (10), Selah (7), Esther (2), and Ellie (1). Chelsea is homeschooling their older two kids for the fifth year while wrangling babies and trying to keep PlayDoh out of the carpet.

Tobi Henschel
Writer/Editor
Tobi and her husband, Paul, met at Moody Bible Institute and have been serving in churches together since then. Along with their three amazing boys, they currently serve in the middle of Illinois farmland at a church where Paul is the senior pastor. Tobi has a passion for teaching the Word of God, especially to children, and helps with both the children's and women's ministries of her church. She loves reading, DIY projects, coffee, ice cream, and spontaneous dance parties with her boys.

Sue Hoijer
Editor of Love, Joy & Faithfulness: a 90-Day Devotional
Sue is a P.K. originally from Minnesota, but she has lived in Michigan's Upper Peninsula since she was 16. After graduating from Bob Jones University, Sue married the carpenter she'd gotten to know during church workdays on a building addition. In 1992, she and her husband were part of a church plant in Marinette, Wisconsin, and they have served in various ministries at that church since then. She enjoys freelance editing, especially when the projects are ministry-related; walking on country roads with her husband, John, and their three daughters; reading; and lilacs and peonies.

Sarah Johnson
Writer
Sarah has been a pastor's wife in the Upper Peninsula of Michigan and in Utah County, the center of Mormonism. She can't think of two more opposite places in the US, but each has been a special joy. She has six children and spends most of her time homeschooling and ministering alongside her husband at Fellowship Bible Church in Pleasant Grove, Utah. Sarah loves the great outdoors and feeding people and agrees with C.S. Lewis that "you can never get a cup of tea large enough or a book long enough to suit me."

Cara Kipp
Writer/Editor/Social Media Manager
Cara and her husband, Adam, have ministered in a small-town church in Illinois for more than a dozen years. The town is small, but sadly not small enough that she can raise chickens. However, she is raising three plucky kids and a six-toed cat. Since being saved as a teenager, she's been involved with the local church, using her passion for women and intergenerational ministry in church planting and church strengthening. She has a passion for Jesus, working out, knitting, and coffee.

Deb Lindstrom
Contributor
Deb Lindstrom has been a pastor's wife for almost 25 years and spent time as a missionary in Romania prior to that. Deb works full-time as a Student Advocate for at-risk students in the local school district and serves with her husband, Jay, at Christ Community Church in Roggen, CO. Jay and Deb have raised four children and have a heart for reaching teens for Christ through their Hey!Loft youth ministry.

Nicole Martin
Writer
Nicole is married to Trevor, who pastors at Calvary Baptist Church in the small town of Emo, Ontario. She grew up in rural Manitoba and attended Briercrest College in Saskatchewan, graduating with a Bachelor of Arts in Christian Ministry. Nicole has opportunities to serve the Lord as she connects with women and families, learns how to support her husband, and perseveres in joyfully mothering their three little ones. They love hosting, seeing neighbours on family walks, and playing board games together. She particularly enjoys the Lord in gardening, baby giggles, a freshly organized drawer, and praying with a friend.

Diane Mathis
Contributor
Diane (Di) Mathis accepted Christ as her Savior during college at the University of Wyoming. However, due to personal sin choices and lack of discipleship, she experienced little growth as a new believer. After five difficult years of marriage, she rededicated her life to Jesus, and her husband Scott was gloriously saved! Two years later God called them into pastoral ministry where they loved serving as a team for 24 years until the Lord re-assigned Scott to become the President of the Berean Fellowship of Churches in 2016. Scott & Di have been married 36 years and have two children and four grandchildren. Di loves hiking and playing with her grandkids.

Jennifer McConnell
Guest Writer
Jason and Jennifer McConnell and their four children live in Franklin, Vermont, where they have served in small-town church ministry for over fifteen years. Jason is the senior pastor of Franklin United Church and East Franklin Union Church. Jennifer leads worship each Sunday and teaches music public elementary schools in Franklin and nearby Sheldon. She earned a Church Music degree from Moody Bible Institute, where she and Jason met. She enjoys networking with other small-town pastors' wives.

Wendy McCready
Assistant Director/Writer
Wendy lives in Alma, Ontario, with her husband, Mark, and two daughters. Mark has been the senior pastor of Alma Bible Church since the summer of 2010. Together they have served for nearly twenty years in rural and small-town pastoral ministry. Wendy works as an educational assistant in the local schools, where she enjoys making community connections in order to share Christ and helping children with special challenges learn new things. She also enjoys

participating in music ministry in their church and hosting people in their home.

Leigh Powers
Guest Writer
Leigh Powers has had a lifelong love affair with the Word of God. A pastor's wife, mother of three, and award-winning author and speaker, she is passionate about helping women find hope and healing in God's Word. She is the author of *Renewed: A 40-Day Devotional for Healing from Church Hurt and for Loving Well in Ministry*. Connect with Leigh on Facebook (@LeighPowersMinistries), Twitter (@leigh_powers), or at her blog www.leighpowers.com)

Lois Seadore
Board of Reference
Lois and her husband, Al, have four grown children, four granddaughters, and one grandson. At present they serve in a church in Marquette, Kansas. She has always loved teaching small groups of women, and God provides opportunities for this ministry. She also enjoys leading worship at a state park ministry. She has asked God to make her a woman of worship in her whole life. She enjoys leading the worship at Marquette and at occasional outreaches. Her biggest joy is interceding for others.

Karen Stiller
Board of Reference, Author/Editor of Faith Today
Karen Stiller is the author of *The Minister's Wife: a Memoir of Faith, Doubt, Friendship, Loneliness, Forgiveness and More* (Tyndale House, 2020), a senior editor of *Faith Today* magazine, and hosts Faith Today Podcast. She is co-author of a number of other books. Karen is married to Brent Stiller, a priest with the Anglican Church in North America. They live in Ottawa and have three adult children, Erik, Holly and Thomas. You can learn more about Karen at www.karenstiller.com.

Ellen Tuttle

Board of Reference

Ellen Tuttle is a wife, mom, grandmother, teacher, speaker, and former pastor's wife. She and her husband, Phil, pastored in Illinois for seven years before joining the staff of Walk Thru the Bible in 1992. Phil has been President of Walk Thru the Bible since 2007. Ellen retired from teaching high school and stays busy traveling internationally with Phil. She speaks and occasionally writes. She left a piece of her heart in their small-town church and still considers herself a pastor's wife, so she loves to pray for rural ministry!

Stacey Weeks

Author/Speaker/Guest Writer

Stacey and her husband, Kevin, serve the Lord in Brantford, Ontario, at Mission City Bible Church, where her husband is the lead pastor. She wrote *Glorious Surrender* to help other ministry wives discover that some of God's greatest blessings are found in those parts of our lives that are most difficult to surrender. Find out more about Stacey and her teaching ministry at StaceyWeeks.com.

Made in the USA
Monee, IL
11 June 2021

71022036R00138